Schülerhilfe®
Das Original. Seit 1974.

Testbuch ENGLISCH

5.–6. Klasse

W0392049

Bildquellen
Stift S K Chavan/Shutterstock.com – **S. 7** fuyu liu/Shutterstock.com – **S. 16** isak55/Shutterstock.com – **S. 25** danielo/Shutterstock.com – **S. 55** KimSongsak/Shutterstock.com – **S. 64** iStock.com/malerapaso – **S. 76** 2jenn/Shutterstock.com – **S. 82** Alexey Wraith/Shutterstock.com – **S. 91** ChristianChan/Shutterstock.com – **S. 94** Pisit Koolplukpol/Shutterstock.com; TanyaRozhnovskaya/Shutterstock.com; Look Studio/ Shutterstock.com; – **S. 106** jesadaphorn/Shutterstock.com – **S. 118** Mr Doomits/Shutterstock.com

www.schuelerhilfe.de

Herausgeber: ZGS Bildungs-GmbH, Gelsenkirchen
Redaktionsleitung: ZGS Bildungs-GmbH, Gelsenkirchen
Layout: Maria Mandelkow, zweiband.media, Berlin
technische Umsetzung: zweiband.media, Berlin
Lektorat/Korrektorat: ZGS Bildungs-GmbH, Gelsenkirchen
Umschlaggestaltung: Trapps Team für Kommunikation GmbH, Hamburg
Umschlagabbildung: ZGS Bildungs-GmbH, Gelsenkirchen

Liebe Schülerin, lieber Schüler!

„Übung macht den Meister."

Du kennst dieses Sprichwort. Beim ersten Mal Lesen sagst du „ja, das stimmt".

Doch dann kommen dir Zweifel: Üben kostet doch Zeit, ist anstrengend, und eigentlich weiß ich doch Besseres mit meiner Zeit anzufangen. Ja, auch das mag stimmen. Doch mit einem kleinen Trick kann das Üben sogar Spaß machen. Der Trick besteht erstens darin, in kleinen Portionen zu üben, und zweitens, dieses regelmäßig zu tun.

In dem vorliegenden Testbuch haben deine Trainer diesen Trick eingebaut: Du findest pro Seite eine kleine Lernportion, die du bearbeitest – sehr überschaubar und frei nach dem Motto „In der Kürze liegt die Würze".

Für die richtigen Lösungswege kannst du dir Musteraufgaben auch online ansehen.

Suche dir einfach die für dich passendste Lernalternative aus – eine wirklich innovative Art des Lernens! Dabei sind die Tests überschaubar, vermitteln dir die Lerninhalte sehr anschaulich und motivieren dich zum Lernen.

Der wichtigste Vorteil ist, dass ein solches Lernen wenig Zeit beansprucht. Das Schülerhilfe-Testbuch eignet sich also ideal, mehrmals wöchentlich eine kleine Übungseinheit einzubauen. Du wirst sehen: Damit kommt Langeweile gar nicht erst auf, und du schaffst es ganz leicht mäßig, aber regelmäßig zu üben!

Wenn du zum Beispiel täglich nach den Hausaufgaben noch eine Seite aus dem Testbuch bearbeitest, ist das das ideale Zusatztraining, um deine Noten langfristig zu verbessern. Wichtig ist, dass du dich nicht überforderst! Ein Üben mit dem Testbuch nach dem Motto „mäßig, aber regelmäßig" frisst keine wertvolle Freizeit, und die Anstrengung hält sich auch in Grenzen. Denn Lernen soll schließlich Spaß machen!

Viel Spaß und Erfolg bei deinen Trainingseinheiten!

Prof. Dr. Ludwig Haag
Lehrstuhl für Schulpädagogik
Kulturwissenschaftliche Fakultät der Universität Bayreuth
Mitglied des Pädagogischen Beirats der Schülerhilfe Deutschland

QUALITÄTSZERTIFIKAT DER UNIVERSITÄT BAYREUTH
DIE IDEALE LERN-KOMBINATION

PÄDAGOGISCH SINNVOLL
EMPFOHLEN VOM LEHRSTUHL FÜR SCHULPÄDAGOGIK

Dr. L. Haag

Zur Arbeit mit diesem Buch

Dieses Testbuch ist die ideale **Übungsergänzung** zur **Lernhilfe** „Gute Noten mit der Schülerhilfe“ Englisch Klasse 5/6.
Sie bietet dir über **250 Tests** im Buch & online zu genau deinen Englisch-Themen, die du gerade im Unterricht behandelst: hiermit kannst du dein Wissen festigen und dieses in zusätzlichen Übungen trainieren.

Dieses Übungsbuch ist eine Kombination aus Buch- und digitalen Lerninhalten, das ideal auf deine Schulinhalte abgestimmt ist.

Es bietet dir zusätzlich zur Lernhilfe:

- thematisch aufgebaute **Tests in 3 Schwierigkeitsstufen**
  Zeichenerklärung: ■□□ = leicht, ■■□ = mittel, ■■■ = schwierig
- alle **Lösungen** zu allen Testaufgaben hinten im Anhang
- einen themenübergreifenden **Abschlusstest** am Ende des Buches

So arbeitest du am besten mit diesem Testbuch:

1. SCHRITT Beginne mit Test 1 des Testbuches und probiere alle Aufgaben selbstständig zu lösen.

2. SCHRITT Nachdem du den Test vollständig bearbeitet hast, bewerte nach den Lösungen im Anhang, wie viele Aufgaben du richtig gelöst hast und vergebe hierfür Punkte, die du in die Punktekästen auf jedem Testblatt eintragen kannst.

3. SCHRITT Hast du 80 % der Punkte eines Tests erreicht (Die genaue Anzahl der Punkte ist immer ganz unten auf jeder Testseite angegeben.), gehe weiter zum nächsten Test. Bei weniger erreichten Punkten wiederhole den Test noch einmal.

4. SCHRITT Bei Problemen mit den Aufgaben stehen dir zahlreiche Musteraufgaben zu vielen Aufgabentypen im Online-LernCenter zur Verfügung, die dir exemplarisch den richtigen Lösungsweg noch einmal erklären.

Wenn du alle Tests im Buch zu deinem Thema gelöst hast, findest du weitere **Übungsaufgaben, Lernvideos und Erklärungen** in digitaler Form im Online-Lerncenter der Schülerhilfe. Der **QR- und der Webcode** auf jeder Testseite führen dich direkt auf die richtige Seite im Online-Lerncenter.

Du hast hier 2 Möglichkeiten, so funktioniert es:

1. **Scanne den QR-Code,** den du auf deiner Testseite unten findest. Du wirst dann direkt zu deinem Thema in das Online-Lerncenter geleitet. Hier kannst du dann zusätzliche Aufgabenblätter zum Üben herunterladen, dir Lernvideos ansehen oder Erklärungen zum Thema nachlesen.

2. Gehe auf die Seite **www.schuelerhilfe.de/gute-noten** und gib dann den **4-stelligen Webcode,** den du unten auf deiner Testseite findest, in das vorgesehene Eingabefeld ein. Du wirst dann im Online-Lerncenter direkt zu deinem Thema weitergeleitet.

Inhaltsverzeichnis

1 Die Zeiten – Das Present Tense

1.1 Aussagesätze (**Test 1–3**) ... 7
1.2 Fragesätze (**Test 4–6**) ... 10
1.3 Verneinte Sätze (**Test 7–9**) ... 13

2 Die Zeiten – Das Present Progressive

2.1 Aussagesätze (**Test 10–12**) ... 16
2.2 Fragesätze (**Test 13–15**) ... 19
2.3 Verneinte Sätze (**Test 16–18**) ... 22

3 Die Zeiten – Das Past Tense

3.1 Das Verb to be im Simple Past (**Test 19–24**) ... 25
3.2 Die regelmäßigen Verben (**Test 25–30**) ... 31
3.3 Die unregelmäßigen Verben (**Test 31–36**) ... 37
3.4 Aussagesätze (**Test 37–42**) ... 43
3.5 Fragesätze (**Test 43–45**) ... 49
3.6 Verneinte Sätze (**Test 46–48**) ... 52

4 Die Zeiten – Das Past Progressive

4.1 Aussagesätze (**Test 49–51**) ... 55
4.2 Fragesätze (**Test 52–54**) ... 58
4.3 Verneinte Sätze (**Test 55–57**) ... 61

5 Die Zeiten – Das Present Perfect

5.1 Aussagesätze (**Test 58–60**) ... 64
5.2 Fragesätze (**Test 61–63**) ... 67
5.3 Verneinte Sätze (**Test 64–66**) ... 70
5.4 Stellung der Adverbien beim Present Perfect (**Test 67–69**) ... 73

6 Die Zeiten – Future Tenses

6.1 Das *going-to*-Future (**Test 70–72**) ... 76
6.2 Das *will*-Future (**Test 73–75**) ... 79

Inhaltsverzeichnis

7 Der Gebrauch der verschiedenen Zeiten
7.1 Simple Present oder Present Progressive **(Test 76–78)** 82
7.2 Simple Past oder Past Progressive **(Test 79–81)** 85
7.3 *will*-Future oder *going-to*-Future **(Test 82–84)** 88

8 Die Verben
8.1 Die modalen Hilfsverben *can* und *can't* **(Test 85–87)** 91
8.2 Die modalen Hilfsverben *must* und *needn't* **(Test 88–90)** 94
8.3 Die modalen Hilfsverben *may* und *might* **(Test 91–93)** 97
8.4 Das Verb *to be* **(Test 94–96)** 100
8.5 Der Imperativ **(Test 97–99)** 103

9 Die Pronomen
9.1 Die Personalpronomen: Subjekt- und Objektform **(Test 100–102)** 106
9.2 Die Possessivpronomen **(Test 103–105)** 109
9.3 Demonstrativpronomen **(Test 106–108)** 112
9.4 Die Reflexivpronomen **(Test 109–111)** 115

10 Abschlusstest **(Test 112)** 118

11 Lösungen 121

Test 11 Aussagesätze

Schwierigkeitsgrad

A1 Setze die Verben im *Present Progressive* ein. 5

a) Mary *(to read)* at the library.

b) My girlfriend *(to watch)* TV right now.

c) They *(to play)* with their toys.

d) Mrs. Miller *(to clean)* the bathroom.

e) You can't play football at the moment. It *(to storm)*.

A2 Übersetze die Sätze ins Englische. 5

a) Er liest gerade die Zeitung.

b) Wir spielen gerade mit dem Ball.

c) Sie kaufen gerade Karten für das Kino.

d) Jane und Jenny spülen gerade das Geschirr ab.

e) Mr. Miller wäscht gerade sein Auto.

A3 Schreibe die Satzteile in der richtigen Reihenfolge. 5

a) A ▪ Rafael ▪ movie ▪ watching ▪ is

b) Funny ▪ we ▪ are ▪ game ▪ a ▪ playing

c) Barking ▪ at ▪ the ▪ dog ▪ is ▪ cat ▪ the

d) His ▪ Oliver ▪ pets ▪ is ▪ feeding

e) Philipp and Johnny ▪ singing ▪ a ▪ are ▪ song ▪ wonderful

oder:
www.schuelerhilfe.de
/gute-noten
CODE 6405

bearbeitet am | zu erreichende Punktzahl: 15 | erreichte Punktzahl des Schülers

➨ Ab 12 erreichten Punkten kannst du zum nächsten Test übergehen.

Test 12 Aussagesätze

Schwierigkeitsgrad

A1 Schreibe die Verben in der *Present Progressive* Form. 6

a) Andrew and my mother *(to bake)* muffins.

....

b) Paul *(to write)* a letter.

....

c) Alexander *(to dance)* with his wife Angelika.

....

d) They *(to take)* a shower.

....

e) I *(to save)* money for a new computer game.

....

f) He *(to cut)* the grass.

....

A2 Entscheide zwischen *Simple Present* und *Present Progressive*. 14

a) Hello. Amy is my Sister. Look! She .... *(to go)* to school.

b) She .... *(to wear)* a raincoat and wellies and she .... *(to carry)* an umbrella.

c) Amy usually .... *(to cycle)* to school, but today she .... *(to take)* the bus because it .... *(to rain)*.

d) The bus .... *(to leave)* at 7.00 and .... *(to arrive)* at Amy's school at 7.50.

e) The first lesson .... *(to begin)* at 8 o'clock. We .... *(to live)* in a little village. This week, I .... *(to do)* a practical course in a bank.

f) I usually .... *(to wear)* jeans and t-shirts but as I .... *(to work)* for the bank now, I .... *(to wear)* a suit and a tie.

oder:
www.schuelerhilfe.de/gute-noten
CODE 6405

bearbeitet am | zu erreichende Punktzahl: 20 | erreichte Punktzahl des Schülers

➨ Ab 16 erreichten Punkten kannst du zum nächsten Test übergehen.

Test 13 Fragesätze

Schwierigkeitsgrad

A1 **Fülle die Lücken aus.** 14

Are Pia and Max playing a game? *(yes)*

a) .... Sofie watching a movie? *(no)*

b) .... your parents sleeping? *(no)*

c) .... you going to school? *(yes)*

d) .... she eating spaghetti? *(yes)*

e) .... we going to the cinema? *(yes)*

f) .... he talking to you? *(no)*

g) .... you learning English? *(no)*

Beantworte nun die obenstehenden Fragen. Die richtigen Antworten stehen in Klammern dahinter.

Yes, they are

h) ....

i) ....

j) ....

k) ....

l) ....

m) ....

n) ....

A2 **Bilde Fragen mit den vorgegebenen Satzteilen.** 4

a) flying / is / to America / she

....

b) are / eating / pizza / you

....

c) crying / is / to cry / he

....

d) they / listening / are / a CD

....

oder:
www.schuelerhilfe.de/gute-noten
CODE 1913

bearbeitet am | zu erreichende Punktzahl: 18 | erreichte Punktzahl des Schülers

➡ Ab 14 erreichten Punkten kannst du zum nächsten Test übergehen.

Test 14 Fragesätze

Schwierigkeitsgrad

A 1 Forme die Sätze in Fragen um. 7

a) I am reading a book.

....

b) We are eating a pizza.

....

c) They are looking tired.

....

d) She is playing with her teddy.

....

e) He is watching a football match.

....

f) My mum is taking a shower.

....

g) Dad is repairing our car.

....

A 2 Bilde Fragen aus den vorgegebenen Satzteilen. 6

a) to ride a horse / my sister

....

b) to play football / my brother

....

c) I / the cinema / to go to

....

d) to buy / fruits / mum / at the supermarket

....

e) to brush our teeth / in the bathroom / we

....

f) spaghetti / to eat / we

....

oder:
www.schuelerhilfe.de
/gute-noten
CODE 1913

bearbeitet am | zu erreichende Punktzahl: 13 | erreichte Punktzahl des Schülers

➨ Ab 10 erreichten Punkten kannst du zum nächsten Test übergehen.

Test 15 Fragesätze

Schwierigkeitsgrad

A1 Erstelle Fragen aus den vorgegebenen Satzteilen. 7

a) your sister • to search • a new • for • house

……………………………………

b) to wear • trousers • you • or a skirt • today

……………………………………

c) to visit • Lisa • her boyfriend

……………………………………

d) with your • grandparents • to talk • about important things • you

……………………………………

e) Otto • comics • to read • or books

……………………………………

f) to take • or the bus • the car • he

……………………………………

g) to eat • outside • they • because • summer • it's

……………………………………

A2 Fülle den Lückentext aus. 16

a) Mr. Smith: Hi, ……………, *(to be)* you ready to go to the restaurant?
Mrs. Smith: Yes, I ……………. I …………… …………… *(to come)* to your car now. …………… you …………… *(to wait)* for me?
Mr. Smith: Oh yes, I …………… …………… *(to wait)* for you. You …………… …………… *(to look)* great tonight.

b) Our family …………… *(to be)* in the garden today. The sun …………… …………… *(to shine)* and the children …………… …………… *(to have)* fun. My mum …………… …………… *(to look)* after the flowers and my dad …………… …………… *(to read)* the newspapers. My siblings …………… …………… *(to play)* badminton. Bello, our dog …………… …………… *(to sleep)* in the sun.

c) In the zoo a little fish …………… …………… *(to swim)* in the aquarium.
A monkey …………… …………… *(to climb)* up a tree and another monkey …………… …………… *(to play)* with the baby monkey.

oder:
www.schuelerhilfe.de/gute-noten
CODE 1913

bearbeitet am | zu erreichende Punktzahl: 30 | erreichte Punktzahl des Schülers

➡ Ab 24 erreichten Punkten kannst du zum nächsten Test übergehen.

Test 16 Verneinte Sätze

Schwierigkeitsgrad

A1 Kreuze die richtige Form an. (6)

a) They ☐ aren't / ☐ 'm not watching a movie.

b) She ☐ aren't / ☐ isn't calling my sister.

c) The sun ☐ isn't / ☐ 'm not shining today.

d) We ☐ aren't/ ☐ isn't talking.

e) Our English teacher ☐ isn't / ☐ aren't teaching Spanish.

f) I ☐ 'm not / ☐ isn't flying to Africa.

A2 Was machen sie NICHT? Fülle die Lücken mit der richtigen Verneinung. (8)

a) My family .... *(go)* outside today.

b) They .... *(play)* tennis.

c) Klara .... *(watch)* TV.

d) I .... *(ride)* my bike.

e) We .... *(buy)* new clothes.

f) Grandma .... *(look)* very old.

g) I .... *(wear)* a skirt today.

h) He .... *(cook)* spaghetti.

A3 Bilde aus den vorgegebenen Satzteilen Sätze, was die Personen gerade NICHT machen. (8)

a) Mika / sleep: ....

b) My sister / brush her teeth: ....

c) Grandpa / read the newspaper: ....

d) We / draw a picture: ....

e) I / go to bed: ....

f) Dad / repair the car: ....

g) Mum / watch a movie: ....

h) Felix / take a shower: ....

oder:
www.schuelerhilfe.de
/gute-noten
CODE 4421

bearbeitet am | zu erreichende Punktzahl: 22 | erreichte Punktzahl des Schülers

➨ Ab 17 erreichten Punkten kannst du zum nächsten Test übergehen.

Test 17 Verneinte Sätze

Schwierigkeitsgrad

A1 **Fülle die Lücken mit den angegebenen Wörtern aus. Verwende das *Present Progressive.*** 6

a) The teacher isn't writing *(not / write)* on the board.

b) Paula isn't doing *(not / do)* Yoga.

c) I 'm not calling *(not / call)* my mother.

d) He isn't plaing *(not / play)* football.

e) Sara isn't meeting *(not / meet)* Luisa again.

f) They aren't learning *(not / learn)* English.

A2 **Bilde die Verneinung.** 6

a) We are looking for a new house. aren't looking

b) They are helping in the garden. aren't helping

c) She is playing with her cat. isn't playing

d) I am driving to the city. I'm not driving

e) He is relaxing in the sun. isn't relaxing

f) She is closing the door. isn't closing

A3 **Forme diese Sätze ins *Present Progressive* um.** 6

a) We don't go home now. We aren't going home now.

b) They don't work today. They aren't working today.

c) I don't love you. I'm not loving you.

d) My parents don't watch TV. My parents aren't watching TV.

e) Kira doesn't cry. Kira isn't crying.

f) Tom doesn't visit a restaurant. Tom isn't visiting a restaurant.

oder:
www.schuelerhilfe.de
/gute-noten
CODE 4421

bearbeitet am | zu erreichende Punktzahl: 18 | erreichte Punktzahl des Schülers

➨ Ab 14 erreichten Punkten kannst du zum nächsten Test übergehen.

Test 18 Verneinte Sätze

Schwierigkeitsgrad

A1 **Setze die richtige Form von „to be“ (verneinte Form) und das Verb ein.** 10

a) My class .... *(buy)* a present for my birthday but I .... *(be)* sad about it. We .... *(celebrate)* my birthday in a restaurant, we are staying at home. My friends are coming but my grandma .... *(come)* because she's ill.

b) My sister .... *(sit)* on the sofa. She is talking to her boyfriend in the kitchen, but they .... *(cook)*. They .... *(be)* hungry.

c) Right now, Ben and Anna are eating breakfast. Anna .... *(drink)* coffee. Anna prefers tea. Ben .... *(drink)* tea. They are eating cornflakes but they .... *(have)* milk.

A2 **In den Text haben sich Fehler eingeschlichen. Verbessere die Fehler. Neben jedem Satz findest du Platz, sie zu korrigieren.** 6

a) The children isn't at home. They are at school. ....

b) Mika isn't learn Englisch, he is practicing German. ....

c) Lina aren't sitting on the chair, she is sitting on the desk. ....

d) The teacher isn't see it. ....

e) After school Mika and Lina isn't going home. ....

f) They are visit their grandparents. ....

A3 **Setze die Satzteile in einen vollständigen Satz zusammen. Verwende außerdem das Present Progressive und passe die Verben an.** 2

a) She / play / computer / not / is / because / not / well / feel

....

b) They / drive / are / not / their / because / car / dad / repair / is / it

....

oder:
www.schuelerhilfe.de
/gute-noten
CODE 4421

bearbeitet am | zu erreichende Punktzahl: 18 | erreichte Punktzahl des Schülers

➨ Ab 14 erreichten Punkten kannst du zum nächsten Test übergehen.

Die Zeiten – Das Past Tense

LERNEINHEIT 3

Test 19 Das Verb *to be* im Simple Past

Schwierigkeitsgrad

A1 Fülle die Lücken, indem du die richtige Form von *to be* im *Simple Past* einträgst. 8

a) 1. Pers. Sg.: I was

b) 2. Pers. Sg.: You were

c) 3. Pers. Sg.: He / She / It was

d) 1. Pers. Pl.: We were

e) 2. Pers. Pl.: You were

f) 3. Pers. Pl.: They were

g) Verneinung: I / He / She / It wasn't

You *(Sg.)* / We / You *(Pl.)* / They weren't

A2 Verwende die richtige Form von *to be* im *Simple Past*. 5

a) My mum was very tired yesterday.

b) They were really nice people.

c) We were at home the whole weekend.

d) Anton was rude to his brother.

e) You were ten years old when we moved to our new house.

A3 Setze die richtige Form von *to be* ein, um die Fragen und Aussagen zu vollenden. 7

a) Were they from Philadelphia?

b) No, she was having a good time. She had a cold.

c) No, we were in love. We just liked each other a lot.

d) Was he supposed to be there that day?

e) No, he was at home yesterday.

f) Were you about to ask something?

g) No, it was cold. The sun was shining.

oder: www.schuelerhilfe.de/gute-noten CODE 2655

bearbeitet am | zu erreichende Punktzahl: 20 | erreichte Punktzahl des Schülers

➨ Ab 16 erreichten Punkten kannst du zum nächsten Test übergehen.

Test 20 Das Verb *to be* im Simple Past

Schwierigkeitsgrad

A 1 **Vervollständige den Lückentext, indem du die richtige Form von *to be* im *Simple Past* einsetzt.** 10

Last August we were on holiday in America. It was an amazing holiday even though my family were in a pretty bad hotel. The rooms were not nice and very dirty, but all the people were really friendly. The food in the restaurant was okay, but the soup was cold. And the ice cream was melted, too. But I was by the ocean every day, and my parents were at the beach, too.

A 2 **Verwende die richtige Verneinung von *to be* im *Simple Past*.** 5

a) Amy wasn't in school.
b) Michael and Michaela weren't in the hotel.
c) I wasn't late.
d) Klaus wasn't in the shop.
e) My parents weren't on the computer.

A 3 **Bilde Fragen im *Simple past*, indem du die Wörter in die richtige Reihenfolge bringst.** 10

a) Was Amy at school today?
b) Were they at the park?
c) Were we away for that weekend?
d) .... that the day we almost had an accident?
e) Was it snowing?
f) Were Stefan and Susanne also there?
g) Was it a very hot day?
h) Were you both 18 when you met?
i) Was the sun already out?
j) Was the baby there yet?

oder:
www.schuelerhilfe.de
/gute-noten
CODE 2655

bearbeitet am | zu erreichende Punktzahl: 25 | erreichte Punktzahl des Schülers

Ab 20 erreichten Punkten kannst du zum nächsten Test übergehen.

Test 21 Das Verb *to be* im Simple Past

Schwierigkeitsgrad

A1 **Vervollständige die Fragen und Antworten mit der richtigen Form von *to be* im *Simple Past*.** | 8

a) Where was Lucia yesterday? – She was at home.

b) Was his dog with him? – No, he wasn't. He was at the park.

c) Were her sisters there, too? – No, they weren't. They were at school.

d) Why wasn't she at school? – She wasn't at school because she was sick.

e) Was Tim at Lisa's party? – No, he wasn't. He was with Justin and Franziska. They were at the cinema.

f) Was he there last Christmas? – Yes, he was.

g) Were they away last holiday? – No, they weren't. They were at home.

h) Were they in Spain all together? – No, they weren't. Andre wasn't with them.

A2 **Kreuze die richtigen Antworten im *Simple Past* an. Es können pro Aufgabe bis zu zwei Antworten richtig sein.** | 4

a)
- ☐ Were she there?
- ☒ Was she there?
- ☐ Weren't she there?
- ☒ Wasn't she there?

b)
- ☒ Were they there?
- ☒ Have they been there?
- ☐ Are they there?

c)
- ☒ Were we there?
- ☐ Was we there?
- ☒ Weren't we there?
- ☐ Wasn't we there?

d)
- ☒ She was there but they weren't.
- ☐ She were there but they were.
- ☐ She was there but they were.
- ☒ She wasn't there but they were.

oder:
www.schuelerhilfe.de
/gute-noten
CODE 2655

bearbeitet am | zu erreichende Punktzahl: 12 | erreichte Punktzahl des Schülers

➡ Ab 10 erreichten Punkten kannst du zum nächsten Test übergehen.

Test 22 Das Verb *to be* im Simple Past

Schwierigkeitsgrad

A 1 Fülle die Lücken mit der richtigen Form des Verbs to be im *Simple Past*. 9

a) Yesterday I was in a nice Italian restaurant with my sister.

b) My brother was busy with a meeting of his company.

c) That's why my brother was not able to join us.

d) We had a nice evening and were very happy.

e) My sister's boyfriend was not invited to the dinner.

f) He was very sad about it.

g) However, it was a family dinner only.

h) Afterwards, my sister and her boyfriend were arguing on the phone about it.

i) She was not happy about it and left.

A 2 Wähle das Wort aus, das grammatikalisch am besten in die Lücke passt. 4

a) Two weeks ago, all my friends ~~were~~ were on holiday.

- 2) were
- 3) are
- 4) aren't

b) I wasn't sure about whether I should go out or stay home tonight.

- 1) am not
- 2) wasn't
- 3) isn't

c) The actors were asked to give an interview about the movie.

- 1) were
- 2) are
- 3) will be

d) My friends were not able to come to the festival, because it was too expensive.

- 1) are not
- 2) will not
- 3) were not

oder:
www.schuelerhilfe.de/gute-noten
CODE 2655

bearbeitet am | zu erreichende Punktzahl: 13 | erreichte Punktzahl des Schülers

➡ Ab 10 erreichten Punkten kannst du zum nächsten Test übergehen.

Test 23 Das Verb *to be* im Simple Past

Schwierigkeitsgrad

A1 Beantworte die Fragen mit der richtigen Form von *to be* in ganzen Sätzen. 5

a) Was the clothes store still open? (+)
Yes, it was.

b) Who was responsible for the cakes for the picnic? *(Sarah and Jenny)*
Sarah and Jenny was responsible for the cakes for the picnic

c) Were the bananas still on sale at the supermarket? (–)
No, they weren't

d) Did I miss the runway show already? (+, two hours ago)
?

e) Was Ben waiting outside already? (–)
No, he wasn't

A2 Kürze die Form von *to be* ab. 5

a) I was not outside then. I wasn't outside then
b) The children were not playing together. the children weren't playing together
c) They are not happy with the wedding cake. They aren't happy with the wedding c..
d) He was not been on the roller coaster. He wasn't been on the roller coaster
e) She was not ready with the exercise, yet. She wasn't ready with the exercise, yet.

x **A3 Fülle die Lücken mit der richtigen Form von *to be* mit Hilfsverben.** 5

a) When I was a child I wanted to be *(to want to be)* a musical star.
b) On her driver's license test, my sister tryed to be *(to try to be)* very good.
c) He hoped to be *(to hope to be)* elected for president.
d) Yesterday, the bride asked me to be *(to ask me to be)* her bride's maid.
e) I didn't wanted to be *(to want to be)* the jealous ex-girlfriend.

oder:
www.schuelerhilfe.de
/gute-noten
CODE 2655

bearbeitet am | zu erreichende Punktzahl: 15 | erreichte Punktzahl des Schülers

➡ Ab 12 erreichten Punkten kannst du zum nächsten Test übergehen.

Test 24 Das Verb *to be* im Simple Past

Schwierigkeitsgrad

X **A1 Stelle die richtigen Fragen in ganzen Sätzen zu den Antworten.** 4

a) Yes, the cake was sold out already.

Was the cake sold out already?

b) Tom was away with the car tonight.

~~Was Tom~~ Who was away with the car tonight?

c) No, the actors weren't welcomed at the red carpet.

~~Was~~ Were the actors welcomed? at the red carpet tonight?

d) No, I don't know where Ben was last weekend.

Do you know where Ben was last weekend?

A2 Fülle die Lücken mit der richtigen Form von *to be*. 6

a) Who was wearing (*to be wearing; Past Progressive*) the red coat last night?

b) The children were laughing (*to be laughing; Past Progressive*) about the joke.

c) My best friend was (*to be; Simple Past*) very surprised about that present.

d) Don't interrupt me! I was just asking (*to be just asking; Past Progressive*) a question.

e) My cousins were (*to be; Simple Past*) late for the family meeting.

f) Last summer, my aunt was (*to be; Simple Past*) on holiday in China.

A3 Bringe die Wörter in die richtige Reihenfolge, sodass ein korrekter Satz entsteht. 3

a) praised • being • was • for • best • I • piano player • the

I was praised for being the piano player.

b) dad • money • asked • donate • was • to • my • yesterday

Yesterday, my dad was ask to donate money.

c) at • were • children • grandma's • their • last week • the

The children were at thair grandma's last week

oder:
www.schuelerhilfe.de/gute-noten
CODE 2655

bearbeitet am | zu erreichende Punktzahl: 13 | erreichte Punktzahl des Schülers

➨ Ab 10 erreichten Punkten kannst du zum nächsten Test übergehen.

Test 25 Die regelmäßigen Verben

Schwierigkeitsgrad

A1 **Kreuze die Sätze an, die im *Simple Past* stehen.** 3

a) ☒ Sally phoned her uncle.

b) ☐ I have been in Canada.

c) ☒ She had an accident.

d) ☐ His friend has a new car.

e) ☒ The tennis players watched the match.

X **A2** **Bilde von den angegebenen, regelmäßigen Verben das *Simple Past*.** 6

a) walk walked

b) watch watched

c) listen listend

d) dance danced

e) look looked

f) work worked

X **A3** **Wandle die gegebenen Aussagesätze ins *Simple Past* um.** 4

a) I like ice cream.

I liked ice cream.

b) We move to Berlin.

We moved to Berlin.

c) The cats walk on the wall.

the cats walked on the wall

d) Mum cooks a soup.

Mum cooked a soup

oder:
www.schuelerhilfe.de
/gute-noten
CODE 5657

bearbeitet am | zu erreichende Punktzahl: 13 | erreichte Punktzahl des Schülers

➨ Ab 10 erreichten Punkten kannst du zum nächsten Test übergehen.

Test 26 Die regelmäßigen Verben

Schwierigkeitsgrad

A4 **Gib bejahte Antworten auf die folgenden Fragen. Verwende das *Simple Past*.** 4

Beispiel

Did she play volleyball? ➨ Yes, she played volleyball.

a) Did they want popcorn?
➨ Yes, they did

b) Did he work on Friday?
➨ Yes, he did

c) Did we watch the parade?
➨ Yes, we did.

d) Did she like the book?
➨ Yes, she did.

A5 **Bilde aus den gegebenen negativen Sätzen positive Aussagesätze im *Simple Past*.** 3

a) I didn't play soccer.
I played soccer.

b) She didn't ask for help.
She asked for help.

c) They didn't repeat the song.
They repeated the song.

X **A6** **Ergänze die Lücken mit den in Klammern gegebenen Verben im *Simple Past*.** 9

a) Somebody opened *(open)* the window.
b) My aunt arrived *(arrive)* yesterday.
c) Bill was in the football team, because he playd *(play)* very well.
d) The headmaster talked *(talk)* to the parents.
e) He answerd *(answer)* and the police officer questioned *(question)* him.
f) I waited *(wait)* for her because she looked *(look)* for her purse.
g) Mom prepared *(prepare)* a delicious meal.

oder:
www.schuelerhilfe.de/gute-noten
CODE 5657

bearbeitet am | zu erreichende Punktzahl: 16 | erreichte Punktzahl des Schülers

➨ Ab 13 erreichten Punkten kannst du zum nächsten Test übergehen.

Test 27 Die regelmäßigen Verben

Schwierigkeitsgrad

A1 Entscheide, ob die Aussagen richtig oder falsch sind. 3

		richtig	falsch
a)	Im amerikanischen Englisch wird ein *-l* am Wortende verdoppelt, bevor das *-ed* angehängt wird. Beispiel: *travelled*	☐	☒
b)	Endet ein Wort auf *-y* nach einem Konsonanten, wird dies zu *-ie*. Beispiel: *worried*	☒	☐
c)	Der Konsonant nach kurzem, betonten Vokal am Wortende wird verdoppelt. Beispiel: *stopped*	☒	☐

X **A2 Kreuze alle Wörter an, die im *Simple Past* regelmäßig gebildet werden.** 5

a) ☐ do
b) ☐ be
c) ☒ walk
d) ☐ write
e) ☒ cry
f) ☒ dance
g) ☐ sleep
h) ☒ want
i) ☐ fly
j) ☒ like

A3 Bilde anhand der gegebenen Satzbausteine korrekte Aussagesätze im *Simple Past*. Füge alle nötigen zusätzlichen Wörter selbstständig ein. 4

a) zoo ▪ yesterday ▪ the class ▪ visit

~~to Zoo~~ Yesterday, the class visited the zoo

b) a knife ▪ to cut ▪ use ▪ she ▪ a face into the pumpkin

She used a knife to cut a face into the pumpkin.

c) ago ▪ the girls ▪ a cheerleading team ▪ 10 years ▪ dance

10 years ago, the girls dance a cheerleading team

d) change ▪ their lunch ▪ last ▪ the students ▪ week

Last week, the students change their lunch.

oder:
www.schuelerhilfe.de
/gute-noten
CODE 5657

bearbeitet am | zu erreichende Punktzahl: 12 | erreichte Punktzahl des Schülers

➨ Ab 10 erreichten Punkten kannst du zum nächsten Test übergehen.

Test 28 Die regelmäßigen Verben

Schwierigkeitsgrad

A1 **Setze die Verben ins *Simple Past*.** 9

a) to plan planed
b) to walk walked
c) to listen listened
d) to talk talked
e) to cook cooked
f) to play played
g) to learn learned
h) to open opened
i) to jump jumped

A2 **Setze die in den Klammern stehenden Verben ins *Simple Past*.** 12

a) My sister stoped *(to stop)* smoking because it is unhealthy.
b) Yesterday we planed *(to plan)* our journey to the USA.
c) Last Christmas my granny baked *(to bake)* the best cookies.
d) My dad carried *(to carry)* me to the car when my leg was broken.
e) We wanted *(to want)* to go to the beach but it was too cold outside.
f) When I was younger I loved *(to love)* to play with my friends in the garden.
g) I asked *(ask)* my teacher for a new pencil.
h) My mother opened *(to open)* my window because it was quite warm in my room.
i) Tina's brother repaired *(to repair)* her bike last Sunday.
j) Tim talked *(to talk)* to Andy clearly.
k) Kai enjoyed *(to enjoy)* the day at the Movie Park.
l) I missed *(to miss)* playing football.

enjoyed

cry try fly ied

oder:
www.schuelerhilfe.de/gute-noten
CODE 5657

bearbeitet am | zu erreichende Punktzahl: 21 | erreichte Punktzahl des Schülers

➡ Ab 17 erreichten Punkten kannst du zum nächsten Test übergehen.

Test 29 Die regelmäßigen Verben

Schwierigkeitsgrad

X **A1 Welche Schreibweise im *Past Tense* ist korrekt. Kreuze die richtige Antwort an.** 8

a) ☒ carried ☐ carryed ☐ carryd
b) ☐ visitted ☒ visited ☐ visite
c) ☐ laughhed ☐ laughd ☒ laughed
d) ☐ tryd ☐ tryed ☒ tried
e) ☒ spotted ☐ spoted ☐ spottet
f) ☐ fited ☐ fittet ☒ fitted
g) ☒ saved ☐ savd ☐ saveed
h) ☒ hurried ☐ hurryed ☐ hurryd

A2 Ergänze die fehlenden Verben. 7

	Simple Present	Simple Past
a)	to suffer	suffered
b)	to control	controled
c)	to waste	wasted
d)	to close	closed
e)	to swap	swaped
f)	to travel	travelled
g)	to jump	jumped

X **A3 Kreuze die Verben an, die eine unregelmäßige *Simple Past* Form haben.** 7

a) ☒ to win
b) ☒ to spring
c) ☒ to wear
d) ☐ to dial
e) ☐ to introduce
f) ☐ to add
g) ☐ to paint
h) ☒ to spend
i) ☒ to swim
j) ☐ to race
k) ☒ to see
l) ☒ to meet

oder:
www.schuelerhilfe.de/gute-noten
CODE 5657

bearbeitet am ___ zu erreichende Punktzahl: 22 erreichte Punktzahl des Schülers ___

➨ Ab 18 erreichten Punkten kannst du zum nächsten Test übergehen.

Test 30 Die regelmäßigen Verben

Schwierigkeitsgrad

A1 **Setze die Sätze ins *Simple Past*.** 6

a) I like the taste of cookies.

I liked the taste of cookies

b) He worries about his sister Miriam.

He worried about his sister Miriam

c) Maggie follows her heart.

Maggie followed her heart

d) My brother Ben reaches the school bus.

My brother Ben reached the school bus

e) Our aunt Claudia wants to move to the Netherlands.

Our aunt Claudia wantted to move to the Netherland

f) I travel to the USA with my boyfriend.

I traveld to the USA with my boyfriend

A2 **Übersetze die folgenden Sätze.** 4

a) Ich habe letzte Woche meine Mutter angerufen.

Last week I called to my mother

b) Gestern habe ich den Klavierunterricht verpasst.

Yesterday I forgot my piano lesson.

c) Mein Vater war nicht über meinen Test erfreut.

My father wasn't amusend about my exam.

d) Gestern hat es den ganzen Tag geregnet.

Yesterday, it rain all day

oder:
www.schuelerhilfe.de/gute-noten
CODE 5657

bearbeitet am | zu erreichende Punktzahl: 10 | erreichte Punktzahl des Schülers

➨ Ab 8 erreichten Punkten kannst du zum nächsten Test übergehen.

Test 31 Die unregelmäßigen Verben

Schwierigkeitsgrad

A1 Kreuze die richtige Form der angegebenen unregelmäßigen Verben im *Simple Past* an. 6

a)	be	☐ are/is	☐ been	☒ was/were
b)	do	☒ did	☐ does	☐ done
c)	have	☐ has	☒ had	☐ hat
d)	go	☐ gone	☒ went	☐ goes
e)	write	☒ wrote	☐ written	☐ writes
f)	see	☐ sees	☒ saw	☐ seen

A2 Schreibe für die angegebenen Verben die Form im *Simple Past* auf. 6

a) win won

b) shut shut

c) let let

d) put put

e) hit hit

f) leave left

A3 Schreibe die gegebenen Sätze in das *Simple Past* um. 4

a) The tree stands next to our house.

?

b) The friends write some letters.

The friends wrote some letters

c) I take the dog for a walk.

I took the dog for a walk

d) The teacher reads a magazine.

The teacher read a magazin

oder: www.schuelerhilfe.de /gute-noten
CODE 0415

bearbeitet am | zu erreichende Punktzahl: 16 | erreichte Punktzahl des Schülers

Ab 13 erreichten Punkten kannst du zum nächsten Test übergehen.

Test 32 Die unregelmäßigen Verben

Schwierigkeitsgrad

X **A1** **Kreuze an, ob die folgenden Sätze korrekt im *Simple Past* stehen.** 5

		richtig	falsch
a)	They were best friends.	☒	☐
b)	Last month Chris did a world tour.	☒	☐
c)	I had sausages for breakfast.	☒	☐
d)	My dad was sitting in the car.	☐	☒
e)	They were singing in the rain.	☐	☒

A2 **Schreibe folgende negative Sätze in positive Aussagesätze im *Simple Past* um.** 5

a) I didn't do my homework.
I did my homework

b) The dogs weren't in the park.
The dogs were in the park.

c) I didn't have lunch yesterday.
I did have lunch yesterday

d) Last night, Dr Thomas didn't sleep well.
Last night, Dr. Thomas did sleep well.

e) My sister didn't buy new jeans.
My sister bought a ~~[illegible]~~ new jeans.

X **A3** **Schreibe für die angegebenen Verben im *Simple Past* die Infinitiv-Form auf.** 6

a) caught catch
b) thought think
c) drove to drive
d) rose rise
e) swam to swimm
f) saw to see

oder:
www.schuelerhilfe.de/gute-noten
CODE 0415

bearbeitet am ______ zu erreichende Punktzahl: 16 erreichte Punktzahl des Schülers ______

➨ Ab 13 erreichten Punkten kannst du zum nächsten Test übergehen.

Test 35 Die unregelmäßigen Verben

Schwierigkeitsgrad

A1 **Ergänze die folgende Tabelle.** 16

X

	Übersetzung	Infinitiv	Past Simple	Past Participle
a)	suchen	search	sought	sought
b)	sinken, untergehen	sink	sank	sunk
c)	zerreißen	to tear	trore	torn
d)	teilen, spalten	to split	slit	split
e)	ausgeben, verbringen	to spend	spent	spent
f)	handeln	to deal	dealt	dealt
g)	graben	to dig	dug	dug
h)	fangen	to catch	caught	caught

X

A2 **Ordne die Verben zu und setze sie in die richtige Zeit.** 9

to eat · to drink · to catch · to do · to forget · to draw · to fall · to forbid · to drive

a) I cought the ball.
b) My mum forgot her key inside the house.
c) I haven't done my homework.
d) Anna has draw a beautiful picture of a sunset.
e) I drawn too much ice cream last night.
f) Yesterday Elli ate too much coffee, so she couldn't sleep well.
g) I haven't drank a car for many years.
h) My parents have driven to use my mobile after 8 p.m.
i) I forbidden in love with him 10 years ago.

oder:
www.schuelerhilfe.de
/gute-noten
CODE 0415

bearbeitet am | zu erreichende Punktzahl: 25 | erreichte Punktzahl des Schülers

➨ Ab 20 erreichten Punkten kannst du zum nächsten Test übergehen.

Test 36 Die unregelmäßigen Verben

Schwierigkeitsgrad

A1 **Ergänze die folgende Tabelle.** 18

	Übersetzung	Infinitiv	Past Simple	Past Participle
a)	aufgehen	to rise	rose	risen
b)	Lesen	to read	read	read
c)	kennen, wissen	to know	knew	known
d)	bauen	to built	built	built
e)	schütteln	to shake	shook	shaken
f)	werfen	to throw	threw	throwen

A2 **Sortiere die Wörter und bilde Sätze im *Simple Past*. Beginne den Satz mit dem jeweils fett geschriebenen Wort.** 6

a) **last** · swim · week · Maggie · Sue · and · sea · the · in

swam

b) take · **it** · to · hours · clean · the floor

took

c) **Dirk** · be · Australia · in · not · has

been

d) write · **Kai** · hundreds · letters · of · me · to · has

written

e) **Heinz** · years · a · many · for · choir · sing · in · has

sung

f) brother · **my** · hide · book · favorite · my

hid

oder:
www.schuelerhilfe.de
/gute-noten
CODE 0415

bearbeitet am | zu erreichende Punktzahl: 24 | erreichte Punktzahl des Schülers

➨ Ab 19 erreichten Punkten kannst du zum nächsten Test übergehen.

LERNEINHEIT 4

Die Zeiten – Das Past Progressive

Test 49 Aussagesätze

Schwierigkeitsgrad

A1 Markiere die Verben im *Past Progressive*. 10

a) We were playing football.

b) Tom was watching television.

c) Sandra was waiting for the bus.

d) The children were buying chocolate.

e) She is playing tennis.

f) They were living in Texas.

g) Sarah was dancing.

h) Sam is standing beside his bike.

i) It was raining.

Wie wird das *Past Progressive* gebildet?

....

A2 Bilde die richtigen Formen der Verben im *Past Progressive*. 11

a) I .... *(to sing)*

b) They .... *(to talk)*

c) You .... *(to live)*

d) He .... *(to swim)*

e) We .... *(to sit)*

f) He .... *(to eat)*

g) She .... *(to leave)*

h) They .... *(to discuss)*

i) It .... *(to rain)*

j) You .... *(to think)*

k) I .... *(to ask)*

A3 Entscheide dich für *was* oder *were*. 8

a) They .... swimming in the pool.

b) She .... watching TV.

c) I .... leaving at 9.30.

d) We .... talking about the movie.

e) He .... drawing.

f) You .... waiting until 3 o'clock.

g) Tom .... playing football.

h) Tim and Sarah .... eating dinner.

oder: www.schuelerhilfe.de/gute-noten
CODE 9485

bearbeitet am ________ zu erreichende Punktzahl: 28 erreichte Punktzahl des Schülers ________

➨ Ab 22 erreichten Punkten kannst du zum nächsten Test übergehen.

Test 50 Aussagesätze

Schwierigkeitsgrad

A 1 **Beschreibe, was die Personen getan haben. Verwende das *Past Progressive*.** 6

a) Cindy *(to draw a picture)*

....

....

b) Grandma Sue *(to drink coffee)*

....

....

c) Baby Ben *(to cry)*

....

....

d) Dad *(to read a paper)*

....

....

e) Usel *(to sleep)*

....

....

f) Evan *(to play with cards)*

....

....

A 2 **Fülle die Lücken mit den richtigen Formen der Verben in Klammern. Verwende *Past Progressive* und *Simple Past*.** 7

a) Sam .... *(to listen)* to music when Tom .... *(to ring)* the doorbell.

b) Tina .... *(to work)* at 9 o'clock.

c) The teacher .... *(to talk)* to the children, when Anna .... *(to come)* in.

d) The children .... *(to play)* football.

e) He .... *(to watch)* television.

oder:
www.schuelerhilfe.de/gute-noten
CODE 9485

bearbeitet am | zu erreichende Punktzahl: 13 | erreichte Punktzahl des Schülers

➨ Ab 10 erreichten Punkten kannst du zum nächsten Test übergehen.

Test 51 Aussagesätze

Schwierigkeitsgrad

A 1 **Benutze die gegebenen Verben, um Sätze im *Past Progressive* zu bilden.** 8

Beispiel

talk / write ➨ They were talking while Anna was writing a letter.

a) listen / dance ....

b) play / hurt ....

c) read / drink ....

d) look / wait ....

e) sit / watch ....

f) think / arrive ....

g) eat / walk ....

h) swim / rain ....

A 2 **Übersetze ins Englische.** 8

a) Die Sonne schien während es regnete.

....

b) Anna war gestern Abend um 9 Uhr arbeiten.

....

c) Sie haben einen Film im Kino geguckt.

....

d) Er hat geschlafen, als sie ihn verließ.

....

e) Das Baby weinte, als die Musik zu laut war.

....

f) Die Sonne schien gestern Morgen.

....

g) Anna träumte, als sie schlief.

....

h) Um 12 Uhr aßen sie.

....

oder:
www.schuelerhilfe.de
/gute-noten
CODE 9485

bearbeitet am | zu erreichende Punktzahl: 16 | erreichte Punktzahl des Schülers

➨ Ab 13 erreichten Punkten kannst du zum nächsten Test übergehen.

Test 52 Fragesätze

Schwierigkeitsgrad

A 1 Bilde die passenden Kurzantworten. | 9

Beispiel

Were they going to the cinema this evening? ➨ Yes, they were.

a) Was it raining? – Yes, ...

b) Were they swimming in the ocean? – Yes, ...

c) Was he watching TV, when she arrived? – Yes, ...

d) Were you leaving work at 6 o'clock? – Yes, ...

e) Was Anna listening to music? – Yes, ...

f) Were they living in France 3 years ago? – Yes, ...

g) Were they sitting around the table, when Peter prepared the dinner? – Yes, ...

h) Was the sun shining? – Yes, ...

i) Was she thinking about leaving him? – Yes, ...

A 2 Ergänze die fehlenden Wörter. | 9

a) .... singing, when you came in? – Yes, she was.

b) .... discussing the topic? – Yes, they were.

c) .... eating? – Yes, he was.

d) .... meeting, when the new member arrived? – Yes, they were.

e) .... leaving at 10 o'clock? – Yes, I was.

f) .... sleeping, when someone called her? – Yes, she was.

g) .... listening to music? – Yes, he was.

h) .... playing football, when their mother came home? – Yes, they were.

i) .... reading the book? – Yes, I was.

A 3 Ergänze die fehlenden Wörter und vervollständige die Antworten. | 8

a) .... you watching TV last evening? – Yes, ...

b) .... Tom driving home, when his mom called him? – Yes, ...

c) .... you leaving at 9.30? – Yes, ...

d) .... she watching the movie? – Yes, ...

e) .... she playing tennis until 5 o'clock? – Yes, ...

f) .... Anna preparing the dinner, when Susanne called her?
– Yes, ...

g) .... you making a phone call, when the accident happened?
– Yes, ...

h) .... Tim and Sophie singing? – Yes, ...

oder:
www.schuelerhilfe.de/gute-noten
CODE 9912

bearbeitet am | zu erreichende Punktzahl: 26 | erreichte Punktzahl des Schülers

➨ Ab 21 erreichten Punkten kannst du zum nächsten Test übergehen.

Test 53 Fragesätze

Schwierigkeitsgrad

A1 Bringe die Wörter in die richtige Reihenfolge und bilde Fragen.

6

a) Writing · letter · she · was · a

b) She · came · was · home · Ben · working · when

c) Was · learning · test · he · the · for

d) The · was · when · started · walk · sun · they · shining · their

e) He · the · leaving · 9 · at · was · office · o'clock

f) Dog · was · when · barking · the · the · came · postman

A2 Verwandle die Aussagesätze in Fragen.

6

a) They were visiting the zoo at 3 o'clock.

b) Sam and Ben were playing soccer, when is started raining.

c) Lisa was reading a book, when the doorbell rang.

d) She was learning for the test.

e) They were cooking together.

f) They were driving on the highway, when the accident happened.

oder:
www.schuelerhilfe.de
/gute-noten
CODE 9912

bearbeitet am | zu erreichende Punktzahl: 13 | erreichte Punktzahl des Schülers

➡ Ab 10 erreichten Punkten kannst du zum nächsten Test übergehen.

Test 54 Fragesätze

Schwierigkeitsgrad

A1 **Stelle dir einen Dialog zwischen zwei Freunden vor. Der eine fragt den anderen über sein Wochenende. Bilde Fragen und Antworten im *Past Progressive*.** 14

a) Were you sleeping, when .... *(parents / prepare / breakfast)*?
– Yes, ...

b) Were you going out, when .... *(start / rain)*? – Yes, ...

c) Were you dancing, when .... *(12 o'clock)*? – Yes, ...

d) Were you doing your homework, when .... *(sun / shine)*?
– No, ...

e) Were you playing football, when .... *(friend / arrive)*? – Yes, ...

f) Were you eating at a restaurant, when .... *(mom / call)*?
– Yes, ...

g) Were you watching a movie, when .... *(fall / asleep)*? – Yes, ...

A1 **Übersetze ins Englische.** 10

a) War Anna am Auto fahren, als ihr Baby anfing zu weinen?
....

b) War sie am Lernen, als ihr Hund spazieren gehen wollte?
....

c) Hast du geschlafen, als ich dich anrief?
....

d) Haben sich Tom und Lena im Café getroffen?
....

e) Hast du am Strand gelegen, als es hier so windig war?
....

f) War sie arbeiten, als ihr Mann krank war?
....

g) Hat er TV geschaut, als sie an der Tür klopfte?
....

h) Waren sie spazieren gehen, als es anfing zu regnen?
....

i) Hat Sam auf den Bus gewartet, als er Anna traf?
....

j) Haben sie gefrühstückt, als sie dich sahen?
....

bearbeitet am ______ zu erreichende Punktzahl: 22 erreichte Punktzahl des Schülers ______

➡ Ab 18 erreichten Punkten kannst du zum nächsten Test übergehen.

Test 55 Verneinte Sätze

Schwierigkeitsgrad

A1 **Fülle die Lücken mit der korrekten Form des Verbs.** 12

a) We .... *(weren't / wasn't)* playing football.

b) It .... *(weren't / wasn't)* raining.

c) She .... *(weren't / wasn't)* listening to the teacher.

d) The children .... *(weren't / wasn't)* leaving school at 5 o'clock.

e) Sam and Tom .... *(wasn't / weren't)* discussing.

f) Anna .... *(wasn't / weren't)* preparing dinner.

g) He .... *(wasn't / weren't)* sitting next to her.

h) She .... *(wasn't / weren't)* thinking about the weather.

i) They .... *(wasn't / weren't)* dancing together.

j) We .... *(wasn't / weren't)* living in Berlin in 1995 yet.

k) You .... *(wasn't / weren't)* reading the book.

l) I .... *(wasn't / weren't)* playing guitar.

A2 **Setze die richtige Form des *Past Progressive* in die Lücken ein.** 12

a) I .... *(not / to leave)* at 9 o'clock.

b) Tim .... *(not / to play)* football.

c) Anna .... *(not / to write)* a letter two hours ago.

d) The baby .... *(not / to sleep)* at night.

e) They .... *(not / to watch)* TV.

f) She .... *(not / to listen)* to the music.

g) Sam .... *(not / to go)* to the theater.

h) He .... *(not / to eat)* the salad.

i) You .... *(not / to wait)* until 3 o'clock.

j) They .... *(not / to talk)* about the book.

k) I .... *(not / calling)* my mother this morning.

l) You .... *(not / to clean)* your room when I entered.

oder:
www.schuelerhilfe.de/gute-noten
CODE 5120

bearbeitet am | zu erreichende Punktzahl: 24 | erreichte Punktzahl des Schülers

➨ Ab 19 erreichten Punkten kannst du zum nächsten Test übergehen.

LE 4: Die Zeiten – Das Past Progressive

Test 56 Verneinte Sätze

Schwierigkeitsgrad

A1 Erstelle aus den folgenden Wörtern verneinte Sätze im *Past Progressive*. 9

a) Sam / play / soccer ....

b) I / have / shower ....

c) she / listen / music ....

d) he / pack / bag ....

e) the children / paint / picture ....

f) my mother / prepare / dinner ....

g) they / discuss / the book ....

h) you / talk / to the teacher ....

i) he / sit / on his chair ....

A2 Beantworte die Fragen mit einer verneinten Antwort im *Past Progressive*. 8

a) Were they having dinner? ....

b) Was she playing tennis? ....

c) Were you wearing a jacket? ....

d) Was he answering your email? ....

e) Were they leaving early? ....

f) Were the kids playing outside? ....

g) Was she using the computer? ....

h) Were they driving to the airport? ....

A3 Finde die Fehler und verbessere sie. Achte auf das *Past Progressive*. 3

a) Sam weren't thinking about the test.

....

b) They wasn't meeting at the café.

....

c) You wasn't reading a book.

....

oder:
www.schuelerhilfe.de
/gute-noten
CODE 5120

bearbeitet am | zu erreichende Punktzahl: 20 | erreichte Punktzahl des Schülers

➨ Ab 16 erreichten Punkten kannst du zum nächsten Test übergehen.

Test 57 Verneinte Sätze

Schwierigkeitsgrad

A1 **Verwende die folgenden Wörter und forme daraus verneinte Aussagesätze.** 5

a) listen · radio · I ……………………………………

b) drink · wine · they ……………………………………

c) read · book · she ……………………………………

d) drive · car · my sister ……………………………………

e) wait · bus · they ……………………………………

A2 **Verwende die folgenden Wörter und forme daraus Fragen im *Past Progressive*. Beantworte dann diese Fragen verneint und ebenfalls im *Past Progressive*.** 10

a) study · test · they

……………………………………

……………………………………

b) swim · pool · your cousin

……………………………………

……………………………………

c) bake · cookies · Sam with Judy

……………………………………

……………………………………

d) eat · pizza · your brothers

……………………………………

……………………………………

e) wear · t-shirt · he

……………………………………

……………………………………

oder:
www.schuelerhilfe.de/gute-noten
CODE 5120

bearbeitet am | zu erreichende Punktzahl: 15 | erreichte Punktzahl des Schülers

➡ Ab 12 erreichten Punkten kannst du zum nächsten Test übergehen.

5 LERNEINHEIT

Die Zeiten – Das Present Perfect

Test 58 Aussagesätze

Schwierigkeitsgrad

A1 Wandle die Verben ins *Present Perfect* um. 8

a) Lena sends ➨ has sent	d) Tina is ➨ has been	g) We invite ➨ have invited
b) My parents talk ➨ have tolked	e) Tom and Tim clean ➨ have cleaned	h) They take ➨ have taken
c) Markus likes ➨ has liked	f) Sara cooks ➨ has cooked	

A2 Entscheide, ob die Sätze richtig oder falsch sind. 7

	richtig	falsch
a) Lina has celebrated her birthday.	☒	☐
b) We have done shopping.	☒	☐
c) She have liked him.	☐	☒
d) He has played football with Mike.	☒	☐
e) They have went to the supermarket.	☐	☒
f) I have bought new clothes.	☒	☐
g) We have were in the cinema.	☐	☒

A3 Setze die richtigen Formen ein. 7

a) We have eaten *(eat)* pizza.

b) I have bought *(buy)* a new t-shirt.

c) The students have forgotten *(forget)* their homework.

d) She has listened *(listen)* her teacher.

e) Tobi has locked *(look)* after his son.

f) My parents have walked *(walk)* with our dog.

g) They have tought *(think)* about summer.

oder:
www.schuelerhilfe.de
/gute-noten
CODE 6254

bearbeitet am | zu erreichende Punktzahl: 22 | erreichte Punktzahl des Schülers

➨ Ab 18 erreichten Punkten kannst du zum nächsten Test übergehen.

Test 59 Aussagesätze

Schwierigkeitsgrad

A1 Vervollständige die Sätze. 8

a) Kim .... already .... *(see)* all Lord of the Rings movies.

b) They .... *(visit)* two supermarkets today.

c) We .... *(eat)* fish today.

d) Lars .... *(go)* to the museum.

e) I .... *(cry)* a lot today.

f) She .... *(drive)* her car.

g) We .... *(make)* lots of mistakes.

h) He .... *(love)* her.

A2 Übersetze ins Deutsche. 5

a) This summer has been hot.

Dieser Sommer war heiß.

b) Sofie has said something.

Sofie hat etwas gesagt.

c) We have cooked something.

Wir haben etwas gekocht.

d) I have worked three days.

Ich habe 3 Tage gearbeitet.

e) They have talked much.

Sie haben viel geredet.

A3 Verwandle die Sätze ins *Present Perfect*. 6

a) I saw a lion in Africa.

....

b) He was a pilot.

....

c) She ate cookies.

....

d) They met the Queen.

....

e) We spent our vacation in Spain.

....

f) I was in Turkey.

....

oder: www.schuelerhilfe.de/gute-noten
CODE 6254

bearbeitet am | zu erreichende Punktzahl: 19 | erreichte Punktzahl des Schülers

➨ Ab 15 erreichten Punkten kannst du zum nächsten Test übergehen.

Test 60 Aussagesätze

Schwierigkeitsgrad

A 1 Vervollständige die Sätze. 6

a) My grandpa isn't at home now. He has gone *(go)* to the supermarket.

b) I know your boyfriend. I have met *(meet)* him already.

c) Our football team has lost *(lose)* all its matches this month.

d) I have seen *(see)* five films with my brother.

e) My mother has taken *(take)* some photos of me.

f) My father has driven *(drive)* to his work.

A 2 Suche dir das passende Verb und vervollständige die Sätze. 6

play · read · meet · find · eat · talk

a) My sister has already read all Harry Potter books.

b) I have found new friends in America.

c) My parents have met their friends today.

d) Leon has played to his mother about school.

e) Sina has talked with her best friend Meike.

f) My family have ate pizza this evening.

Schreiben (Grund!)

A 3 Bringe die Wörter in die richtige Reihenfolge. 5

a) I · homework · already · have · finished · my

b) We · football · have · played · in · the · gym

c) They · have · just · bought · a · car · new

d) She · has · a · movie · watched · today

e) They · talk · have · about · problems · different

oder:
www.schuelerhilfe.de
/gute-noten
CODE 6254

bearbeitet am | zu erreichende Punktzahl: 17 | erreichte Punktzahl des Schülers

➡ Ab 14 erreichten Punkten kannst du zum nächsten Test übergehen.

Test 61 Fragesätze

Schwierigkeitsgrad

A 1 **Setze *has/have* und das Verb in der richtigen Form ein.** 8

a) Have you ever touched *(touch)* a lion?

b) Has she already done *(do)* her homework?

c) Has he got *(get)* your mobile phone?

d) Have they bought *(buy)* new clothes?

e) Have you met *(meet)* her already?

f) Have you been *(be)* in London?

g) Had he asked *(ask)* his grandparents?

h) Had she drawn *(draw)* a picture?

A 2 **Kreuze an, welche Frage richtig im *Present Perfect* gebildet wurde.** 7

a) ☐ She bought a new car?
☒ Has she bought a new car?
☐ Have she bought a new car?

b) ☒ Has he reads a red book?
☐ Did he read a red book?
☐ Has he read a red book?

c) ☒ Have they looked at him?
☐ Have they look at him?
☐ Has they looked at him?

d) ☒ Have we eaten pizza?
☐ We ate pizza?
☐ Did we eat pizza?

e) ☐ Have she gone to New York?
☒ Has she gone to New York?
☐ Did she went to New York?

f) ☐ They flew in a helicopter?
☒ Have they flew in a helicopter?
☐ Have they flown in a helicopter?

g) ☒ Have we cooked for our friends?
☐ Did we cook for our friends?
☐ Cocked we for our friends?

oder:
www.schuelerhilfe.de
/gute-noten
CODE 6920

bearbeitet am | zu erreichende Punktzahl: 15 | erreichte Punktzahl des Schülers

➨ Ab 12 erreichten Punkten kannst du zum nächsten Test übergehen.

Test 62 Fragesätze

Schwierigkeitsgrad

A1 **Bilde die Fragen im *Present Perfect*, indem du die Wörter in der richtigen Reihenfolge anordnest.** 10

a) you · been · ever · have · to · America

....?

b) before · she · has · done · sports

....?

c) he · the · broken · window · has

....?

d) turned · she · has · on · the · radio

....?

e) have · ever · you · watched · horror movie · a

....?

f) travelled · abroad · they · ever · have

....?

g) Marc · been · since when · has · in Scotland

....?

h) your grandparents · already · asked · you · have

....?

i) Mrs. Mann · ever · organized · anything special · has · in school?

....?

j) ever · you · visited · the Eiffel Tower · have

....?

A2 **Fülle die Lücken, indem du das Verb im *Present Perfect* einsetzt.** 8

know · see · be · speak · lose · catch · be · talk

a) Have .... you know .... him for all your life?

b) Have .... they see .... snow before?

c) How long has .... it be .... since you met each other?

d) When have .... we last lose .... ?

e) Has .... she ~~lost~~ catch .... her phone again?

f) Has .... Julius speak .... a cold this year?

g) Where has .... he be .... all my life?

h) Have .... they talk .... to each other for a long time?

oder:
www.schuelerhilfe.de/gute-noten
CODE 6920

bearbeitet am | zu erreichende Punktzahl: 18 | erreichte Punktzahl des Schülers

➡ Ab 14 erreichten Punkten kannst du zum nächsten Test übergehen.

Test 63 Fragesätze

Schwierigkeitsgrad

A1 **Wähle das richtige Fragewort aus und setze das Verb im *Present Perfect* in die Frage ein. Jedes Fragewort kommt nur einmal vor.** 8

when · what · where · why · who · whose · which · how

a) .... have you stayed (*stay*) while travelling across Europe?
b) .... has she forgotten (*forget*) to tell you that the party is today?
c) .... has he telled (*tell*) you that he is sick?
d) ~~Wich~~ which car have you used (*use*) this morning?
e) .... long has it been (*be*) since their cat died?
f) .... exercise have you did (*do*) for today?
g) .... has she imaged (*imagine*)?
h) .... have they talked (*talk*) to already?

A2 **Bilde die Fragen im *Present Perfect*.** 8

a) Are you sure about buying the car?
....?

b) When are you at home?
....?

c) What happens at your grandparents' house?
....?

d) Who tells them what not to say?
....?

e) Did you go to school recently?
....?

f) Why didn't you ask for help?
....?

g) Where do you put the trash?
....?

h) Did she have a dog?
....?

oder: www.schuelerhilfe.de/gute-noten
CODE 6920

bearbeitet am | zu erreichende Punktzahl: 16 | erreichte Punktzahl des Schülers

➨ Ab 13 erreichten Punkten kannst du zum nächsten Test übergehen.

Test 64 Verneinte Sätze

Schwierigkeitsgrad

A 1 Verneine die Verben.

10

a) Has cleaned ➨ ....

b) Has watched ➨ ....

c) Have been ➨ ....

d) Have gone ➨ ....

e) Has said ➨ ....

f) Have finished ➨ ....

g) Has arrived ➨ ....

h) Has liked ➨ ....

i) Have heard ➨ ....

j) Have played ➨ ....

A 2 Kreuze an, ob richtig oder falsch und korrigiere falls notwendig.

6

		richtig	falsch	Korrektur
a)	My sister hasn't been in Turkey.	☐	☐	
b)	They hasn't got a Christmas tree.	☐	☐	
c)	We haven't seen you today.	☐	☐	
d)	My parents haven't be lucky.	☐	☐	
e)	My brother hasn't gone to work.	☐	☐	
f)	He hasn't played hockey.	☐	☐	

A 3 Verneine die Sätze mit den Verben in den Klammern.

4

a) My grandma .... *(to clean)* the kitchen.

b) My father .... *(to drive)* with his new car.

c) My grandparents .... *(to cook)* anything.

d) They .... *(to watch)* TV recently.

oder:
www.schuelerhilfe.de
/gute-noten
CODE 0301

bearbeitet am | zu erreichende Punktzahl: 20 | erreichte Punktzahl des Schülers

➨ Ab 16 erreichten Punkten kannst du zum nächsten Test übergehen.

Test 65 Verneinte Sätze

Schwierigkeitsgrad

A 1 Bringe die Wörter in die richtige Reihenfolge. 6

a) I • red • haven't • a • comic ....

b) She • been • hasn't • holiday • on ....

c) They • eaten • haven't • ice cream ....

d) He • hasn't • laughed • my • about • joke ....

e) We • driven • to • haven't • Las Vegas ....

f) I • haven't • looked • her • at ....

A 2 Verwandle die Sätze ins Negative. 6

a) I have seen a lion in Africa. ➨ ....

b) He has been a pilot. ➨ ....

c) They have met the queen. ➨ ....

d) She has eaten cookies. ➨ ....

e) I have been in Australia. ➨ ....

f) I have worked. ➨ ....

A 3 Verwandle ins *Present Perfect* und verneine. 10

a) She watches ➨ ....

b) He plays ➨ ....

c) They look ➨ ....

d) We talk ➨ ....

e) They spend ➨ ....

f) He rides ➨ ....

g) They say ➨ ....

h) She comes ➨ ....

i) We cut ➨ ....

j) He drives ➨ ....

oder:
www.schuelerhilfe.de/gute-noten
CODE 0301

bearbeitet am ______ zu erreichende Punktzahl: 22 erreichte Punktzahl des Schülers ______

➨ Ab 18 erreichten Punkten kannst du zum nächsten Test übergehen.

Test 66 Verneinte Sätze

Schwierigkeitsgrad

A1 Schreibe negative Sätze mit den vorgegebenen Satzteilen. Verwende das *Present Perfect*. 5

a) we · our · work · finish

b) has · lose · book · his · he

c) drive · they · to · family · their

d) to · she · cinema · go · the

e) German · he · study

A2 Suche dir vier Verben aus und schreibe auf, was du bisher noch NICHT gemacht hast. 4

a) fly to the moon
b) see a dragon
c) go to Asia
d) see a superstar
e) play football with your teacher
f) live in a castle

A3 Verwandle die Sätze ins Negative. 6

a) We have been on vacation ➨
b) The children have slept in their bed ➨
c) She has written a story ➨
d) He has forgotten his book ➨
e) I have tidied my room ➨
f) I have waited for the train ➨

oder:
www.schuelerhilfe.de/gute-noten
CODE 0301

bearbeitet am

zu erreichende Punktzahl: 15

erreichte Punktzahl des Schülers

➨ Ab 12 erreichten Punkten kannst du zum nächsten Test übergehen.

Test 67 Stellung der Adverbien beim Present Perfect

Schwierigkeitsgrad

A1 **Kreuze an, ob die Sätze im *Present Perfect* richtig oder falsch sind.** 8

a) He never has been to London. ☐ richtig ☐ falsch

b) He has never been to London. ☐ richtig ☐ falsch

c) I have my homework just done. ☐ richtig ☐ falsch

d) I have just done my homework. ☐ richtig ☐ falsch

e) They haven't yet gone to the dentist. ☐ richtig ☐ falsch

f) They haven't gone to the dentist yet. ☐ richtig ☐ falsch

g) Mom has already been to Tokyo. ☐ richtig ☐ falsch

h) Mom has been already to Tokyo. ☐ richtig ☐ falsch

A2 **Fülle die Lücken mit den Wörtern in Klammern in der richtigen Reihenfolge.** 6

a) The doctor .... the patient. *(already / seen / has)*

b) The sisters .... cards. *(have / just / played)*

c) I .... to the circus. *(gone / have / never)*

d) Nobody .... that to the teacher. *(ever / has / said)*

e) My brother .... his homework this morning. *(finished / has / already)*

f) The bus driver .... in the roundabout. *(carefully / driven / has)*

A3 **Vervollständige die Fragen mit den Wörtern in der richtigen Reihenfolge und Form.** 6

a) Have you .... to the band? *(already / to listen)*

b) Has he .... the president of the USA? *(ever / to meet)*

c) Have the children .... a letter to aunt Sally? *(ever / to write)*

d) Has your friend .... you that email? *(already / to send)*

e) Have the students .... Italian food? *(ever / to eat)*

f) You haven't .... to the USA, have you? *(ever / to be)*

oder:
www.schuelerhilfe.de
/gute-noten
CODE 2455

bearbeitet am | zu erreichende Punktzahl: 20 | erreichte Punktzahl des Schülers

➡ Ab 16 erreichten Punkten kannst du zum nächsten Test übergehen.

Test 68 Stellung der Adverbien beim Present Perfect

Schwierigkeitsgrad

A1 **Entscheide, ob die folgenden Sätze richtig oder falsch im *Present Perfect* stehen.** 5

a) He had never been to Dublin. ☐ richtig ☐ falsch

b) My husband hasn't done the dishes yet. ☐ richtig ☐ falsch

c) We have just finished our training. ☐ richtig ☐ falsch

d) Had they ever listened to Mozart? ☐ richtig ☐ falsch

e) Have the players ever won a game? ☐ richtig ☐ falsch

A2 **Bilde die passenden Fragen zu den gegebenen Antworten im *Present Perfect*.** 4

a) No, I have never been to the USA.

....?

b) Yes, we have just done our homework.

....?

c) Yes, the class has already watched the new movie.

....?

d) No, I haven't written the postcard yet.

....?

A3 **Setze die Verben und Adverbien in Klammern richtig in die gegebenen Sätze ein. Achte darauf, das *Present Perfect* zu verwenden.** 7

a) She .... to do it. *(just / to try)*

b) .... of it? *(never / you / to hear)*

c) The teachers .... me. *(already / to tell)*

d) I .... Susan coming out of the cinema. *(just / to see)*

e) ....? *(yet / your sister / to finish / her homework)*

f) Oh no, the train ....! *(already / to leave)*

g) My mum .... to bake three cakes for Easter. *(easily / to manage)*

oder:
www.schuelerhilfe.de/gute-noten
CODE 2455

bearbeitet am | zu erreichende Punktzahl: 16 | erreichte Punktzahl des Schülers

➨ Ab 13 erreichten Punkten kannst du zum nächsten Test übergehen.

Test 69 Stellung der Adverbien beim Present Perfect

Schwierigkeitsgrad

A 1 **Bilde anhand der Satzbausteine korrekte Sätze im *Present Perfect*.** 3

a) sister ▪ homework ▪ to not do ▪ my ▪ yet ▪ her

....

b) to be ▪ grandparents ▪ already ▪ our ▪ Berlin ▪ to

....

c) never ▪ to write ▪ many children ▪ a letter

....

A 2 **Beantworte die folgenden Fragen mit negativen Aussagesätzen und füge das Adverb *not...yet* richtig ein.** 5

a) Has he already watched the movie?

....

b) Have the cats already caught any birds?

....

c) Have the Carters ever been to New York City?

....

d) Has the school bought new footballs yet?

....

e) Have the friends already played tennis together?

....

A 3 **Kreuze die grammatikalisch richtigen Fragen an.** 2

a) ☐ Have you yet posted the postcards?

b) ☐ Have you already been to Tokyo?

c) ☐ Why haven't you yet washed the dishes?

d) ☐ Has the patient visited the doctor already?

oder:
www.schuelerhilfe.de
/gute-noten
CODE 2455

bearbeitet am | zu erreichende Punktzahl: 10 | erreichte Punktzahl des Schülers

➨ Ab 8 erreichten Punkten kannst du zum nächsten Test übergehen.

6 LERNEINHEIT

Die Zeiten – Future Tenses

Test 70 Das *going-to*-Future

Schwierigkeitsgrad

A1 Vervollständige die Lücken. 6

a) I .... going to write a letter to my uncle.

b) You .... going to see your relatives this weekend.

c) He .... going to do his homework this afternoon.

d) She .... going to sing the new song at the festival.

e) We .... going to go to the theatre.

f) They .... going to meet in front of Susan's house.

A2 Verneine die folgenden Sätze im *going-to-future*. Verwende die Kurzform. 4

a) Sarah is going to write the exam after lunch. ....

b) The neighbours are going to meet for a barbecue. ....

c) My brother is going to play soccer in the garden. ....

d) My classmates are going to learn for maths together. ....

A3 Beantworte die folgenden Fragen im *going-to-future*. 3

a) Are the Smiths going to visit New York City this summer?

Yes, the Smiths are ....

b) Is dad going to listen to his favourite band tonight?

Yes, dad is ....

c) Are Julia and Stefan going to go to the school ball tonight?

No, Julia and Stefan aren't ....

oder:
www.schuelerhilfe.de
/gute-noten
CODE 9876

bearbeitet am | zu erreichende Punktzahl: 13 | erreichte Punktzahl des Schülers

➨ Ab 10 erreichten Punkten kannst du zum nächsten Test übergehen.

Test 71 Das *going-to*-Future

Schwierigkeitsgrad

A1 **Bilde zu den gegebenen Infinitiven sowohl die positive Form als auch die verneinte Form im *going-to-future*.** 5

a)	to be	(+)	he	....	(–)	he	....
b)	to sleep	(+)	they	....	(–)	they	....
c)	to say	(+)	she	....	(–)	she	....
d)	to go	(+)	we	....	(–)	we	....
e)	to hear	(+)	I	....	(–)	I	....

A2 **Beantworte die folgenden Fragen im *going-to-future*. Nutze Langformen.** 4

a) Are you going to pass the exams at the end of the year?

Yes, ...

b) Is the school going to celebrate an anniversary this autumn?

Yes, the school ....

c) Is she going to sing in the choir this semester?

No, ...

d) Is the elephant going to eat fruits for dinner?

No, it ....

A3 **Leite aus den gegebenen Antworten Fragen im *going-to-future* ab.** 4

a) Yes, Clara is going to become 15 years this Friday.

.... ?

b) Yes, my grandparents are going to buy a house at the beach.

.... ?

c) No, the children aren't going to win the match against the champion.

.... ?

d) No, the cat isn't going to jump onto the wall.

.... ?

oder:
www.schuelerhilfe.de/gute-noten
CODE 9876

bearbeitet am | zu erreichende Punktzahl: 13 | erreichte Punktzahl des Schülers

➨ Ab 10 erreichten Punkten kannst du zum nächsten Test übergehen.

Test 72 Das *going-to*-Future

Schwierigkeitsgrad

A1 Entscheide, ob die Aussagen über das *going-to-future* richtig oder falsch sind. 4

a) Das going-to-future wird verwendet, wenn man Vorhersagen oder Vermutungen über die Zukunft macht. ☐ richtig ☐ falsch

b) Das going-to-future wird verwendet um über Absichten und Pläne für die Zukunft zu sprechen. ☐ richtig ☐ falsch

c) Das going-to-future wird für spontane Entscheidungen verwendet. ☐ richtig ☐ falsch

d) Das going-to-future wird mit einer Form von „to be", „going to" und dem Infinitiv des Hauptverbs gebildet. ☐ richtig ☐ falsch

A2 Setze die Verben in Klammern im *going-to-future* ein. 9

a) What .... you .... *(to do)* this evening?

b) Mom .... *(to go)* to her office at 7 o'clock next Monday.

c) Judy's holidays .... *(to be)* planned perfectly.

d) The officer's dog .... *(not / to bark)* loudly.

e) Timothy .... *(to write)* a test in the sports hall this afternoon.

f) My grandparents .... *(not / to stay)* in a hotel when they visit us.

g) .... the plane .... *(to take off)* on time?

h) The music festival .... *(to take)* place in Las Vegas.

i) I can tell you that I .... *(to ask)* Jonas for a date.

A3 Bilde anhand der gegebenen Satzteile Fragen im *going-to-future*. 5

a) to do • night • tomorrow • homework • your • you

............?

b) the dishes • when • dad • to wash

............?

c) how • to solve • the students • the problem

............?

d) the doctor • to call • the hospital

............?

e) to meet • where • the children • this weekend

............?

oder:
www.schuelerhilfe.de
/gute-noten
CODE 9876

bearbeitet am | zu erreichende Punktzahl: 18 | erreichte Punktzahl des Schülers

➨ Ab 14 erreichten Punkten kannst du zum nächsten Test übergehen.

Test 73 Das *will*-Future

Schwierigkeitsgrad

A1 Kreuze an, welche Signalwörter auf das *will-future* zutreffen können. 2

a) ☐ since, for
b) ☐ tomorrow, next month
c) ☐ always, every
d) ☐ last, yesterday
e) ☐ in 2022, the coming year
f) ☐ ever, before

A2 Setze die richtige Form des *will-future* ein. Nutze die Verben in Klammern. 6

a) Julia and I …………………… to them tomorrow. *(to talk)*
b) …………………… you …………………… your father to tidy up the kitchen? *(to help)*
c) They …………………… back by 8:15 pm. *(to be)*
d) …………………… the festival …………………… place this summer? *(to take)*
e) My parents …………………… me for being late. *(to punish)*
f) The Millers …………………… Christmas in Sussex this year. *(to spend)*

A3 Setze die Kurzform des *will-future* für die gegebenen Sätze ein. 5

a) They will read a book. ➨ They …………………… a book.
b) He will not be late. ➨ He …………………… late.
c) She will never learn. ➨ She …………………… never …………………… .
d) We will not sing this song. ➨ We …………………… this song.
e) I will give you the money. ➨ I …………………… you the money.

oder:
www.schuelerhilfe.de
/gute-noten
CODE 5659

bearbeitet am | zu erreichende Punktzahl: 13 | erreichte Punktzahl des Schülers

➨ Ab 10 erreichten Punkten kannst du zum nächsten Test übergehen.

Test 74 Das *will*-Future

Schwierigkeitsgrad

A1 Bilde zu den gegebenen Infinitiven sowohl die positive Form im *will-future* als auch die verneinte Form im *will-future*. 5

a) to be (+) .... (–) ....

b) to sleep (+) .... (–) ....

c) to say (+) .... (–) ....

d) to go (+) .... (–) ....

e) to hear (+) .... (–) ....

A2 Entscheide, ob die Formen des *will-future* in den Beispielsätzen richtig unterstrichen sind. 6

		richtig	falsch
a)	My uncle <u>will come</u> to dinner this evening.	☐	☐
b)	<u>Will you</u> spend your holidays in Italy this year?	☐	☐
c)	He <u>will</u> never <u>know</u>, will he?	☐	☐
d)	You won't <u>leave</u> the room!	☐	☐
e)	We <u>will not pass</u> this difficult exam.	☐	☐
f)	<u>Will</u> the Turners <u>pay</u> the bill tonight?	☐	☐

A3 Entscheide, ob die Aussagen über das *will-future* richtig oder falsch sind. 5

		richtig	falsch
a)	Das will-future wird für Vorhersagen und Vermutungen verwendet.	☐	☐
b)	Das will-future wird durch ***will + Infinitiv*** gebildet.	☐	☐
c)	Für das Hilfsverb ***will*** gibt es keine Kurzform.	☐	☐
d)	Die Langform der Verneinung ***will not + Infinitiv*** wird zu ***won't + Infinitiv*** verkürzt.	☐	☐
e)	Das will-future wird für zukünftige, eindeutig festgelegte Pläne verwendet.	☐	☐

oder:
www.schuelerhilfe.de
/gute-noten
CODE 5659

bearbeitet am .... zu erreichende Punktzahl: 16 erreichte Punktzahl des Schülers ....

➨ Ab 13 erreichten Punkten kannst du zum nächsten Test übergehen.

Test 75 Das *will*-Future

Schwierigkeitsgrad

A1 **Entscheide, ob das *will-future* in den Beispielen richtig gebraucht wurde.** 6

	richtig	falsch
a) According to the weather report, it ***will*** *be* cloudy tomorrow.	☐	☐
b) Why did you buy this paint? – I ***will*** paint my room tomorrow.	☐	☐
c) Listen! The phone is ringing. – I'***ll*** get it.	☐	☐
d) Sam has just bought a house in York. He ***will*** *move* on Saturday.	☐	☐
e) "Here, I ***will*** *help* you carry that box. It looks heavy."	☐	☐
f) Anna ***will*** *come* tomorrow around 5 o'clock.	☐	☐

A2 **Bilde anhand der vorgegebenen Wörter Fragesätze im *will-future*.** 5

a) *(it / snow)* .... ?

b) *(me / she / forgive)* .... ?

c) *(what / learn / they)* .... ?

d) *(not / the bus / wait / for us)* .... ?

e) *(they / leave / when)* .... ?

A3 **Entscheide, ob das *will-future* in der englischen Übersetzung angebracht ist.** 3

	richtig	falsch
a) Ich schwitze jetzt schon. Es wird heute sehr heiß werden, fürchte ich. ➨ I'm sweating already. It ***will be*** very hot today, I'm afraid.	☐	☐
Ich habe ihm einen Brief auf den Tisch hinterlassen. Glaubst du, dass er ihn finden wird? ➨ I've left a letter for him on the table. Do you think he'***ll see*** it?	☐	☐
b) Früher oder später wird er seinen Fehler bemerken. ➨ Sooner or later he ***will realize*** his mistake.	☐	☐

oder:
www.schuelerhilfe.de/gute-noten
CODE 5659

bearbeitet am | zu erreichende Punktzahl: 14 | erreichte Punktzahl des Schülers

➨ Ab 11 erreichten Punkten kannst du zum nächsten Test übergehen.

7 LERNEINHEIT Der Gebrauch der verschiedenen Zeiten

Test 76 Simple Present oder Present Progressive

Schwierigkeitsgrad

A1 Entscheide, welches Signalwort zu welcher Zeit gehört. Unterstreiche die richtige Antwort. 12

a) Look! *Simple present / present progressive*

b) always *Simple present / present progressive*

c) often *Simple present / present progressive*

d) at present *Simple present / present progressive*

e) usually *Simple present / present progressive*

f) at the moment *Simple present / present progressive*

g) sometimes *Simple present / present progressive*

h) just now *Simple present / present progressive*

i) every day *Simple present / present progressive*

j) now *Simple present / present progressive*

k) on Mondays *Simple present / present progressive*

l) right now *Simple present / present progressive*

A2 Entscheide, welcher Satz richtig ist und markiere diesen mit einem *x*. 9

a) ☐ It is raining right now.
☐ It rains right now.

b) ☐ Sam is often listening to jazz music.
☐ Sam often listens to jazz music.

c) ☐ Anna is visiting her grandma every Sunday.
☐ Anna visits her grandma every Sunday.

d) ☐ They are usually going to Spain.
☐ They usually go to Spain.

e) ☐ At the moment she is eating ice cream.
☐ At the moment she eats ice cream.

f) ☐ They are listening to the teacher right now.
☐ They listen to the teacher right now.

g) ☐ She is being always late.
☐ She is always late.

h) ☐ Listen! Someone is ringing the doorbell.
☐ Listen! Someone rings the doorbell.

i) ☐ She is still listening to the music.
☐ She still listens to the music.

oder:
www.schuelerhilfe.de/gute-noten
CODE 8196

bearbeitet am | zu erreichende Punktzahl: 21 | erreichte Punktzahl des Schülers

➨ Ab 20 erreichten Punkten kannst du zum nächsten Test übergehen.

Test 77 Simple Present oder Present Progressive

Schwierigkeitsgrad

A1 **Ergänze den Lückentext, indem du das Verb entweder im *Simple Present* oder im *Present Progressive* einsetzt.** 13

a) They ………………………… football at the moment. *(to play)*

b) We ………………………… Spanish very often. *(to speak)*

c) She always ………………………… at 5 o'clock. *(to get up)*

d) I never ………………………… the cinema. *(to go)*

e) ………………………… you ………………………… TV right now? *(to watch)*

f) She ………………………… a book at the moment. *(to read)*

g) We ………………………… to Berlin on Friday. *(to go)*

h) She always ………………………… coffee in the morning. *(to drink)*

i) Anja ………………………… guitar every day. *(to play)*

j) They ………………………… soccer every week. *(to watch)*

k) I usually ………………………… to school. *(to go)*

l) They ………………………… dinner right now. *(to prepare)*

m) Listen! She ………………………… guitar. *(to play)*

A2 **Welcher Satz verwendet die richtige Zeitform? Kreuze an.** 8

a) ☐ My mother always picks me up after school.
☐ My mother always is picking me up after school.

b) ☐ She plays tennis right now.
☐ She is playing tennis right now.

c) ☐ He always learns for the test.
☐ He is always learning for the test.

d) ☐ They are now standing in front of the house.
☐ They now stand in front of the house.

e) ☐ She is still crying.
☐ She still cries.

f) ☐ They don't visit us today.
☐ They are not visiting us today.

g) ☐ What are you doing right now?
☐ What do you do right now?

h) ☐ Right now they are dancing.
☐ Right now they dance.

oder:
www.schuelerhilfe.de
/gute-noten
CODE 8196

bearbeitet am ______ zu erreichende Punktzahl: 21 erreichte Punktzahl des Schülers ______

➨ Ab 17 erreichten Punkten kannst du zum nächsten Test übergehen.

Test 78 Simple Present oder Present Progressive

Schwierigkeitsgrad

A1 Vervollständige den Lückentext, indem du die Verben entweder im *Simple Present* oder *Present Progressive* einsetzt. 12

(to) arrive • *(to)* begin • *(to)* leave • *(to)* enjoy • *(to)* visit • *(to)* offer • *(to)* take • *(to)* be • *(to)* want • *(to)* stay • *(to)* take • *(to)* do

Vicky .... to improve her English. That is why she .... a language course in Manchester at the moment. She .... with a very friendly older couple and she must .... the tube to get to her school. Luckily it .... only a two-minute walk to the nearest tube station and the tube that she .... to school .... at quarter past seven. The first lesson .... at 9 o'clock so she usually .... a little early. In the afternoons, the school .... sightseeing tours in and around Manchester and even a weekend trip to London. Tomorrow the students .... the National Football Museum. Vicky .... her time in England very much.

A2 Lies dir die Fragen und Sätze durch und kreuze die richtige Lösung an. 6

a) Wenn eine Uhrzeit durch einen Fahrplan festgelegt ist, verwenden wir:

- ☐ Simple Present
- ☐ Present Progressive

b) Welche Zeitform verwendest du mit folgenden Signalwörtern: ***often***, ***seldom***, ***never***?

- ☐ Simple Present
- ☐ Present Progressive

c) Wenn etwas im Moment des Sprechens stattfindet, verwenden wir:

- ☐ Simple Present
- ☐ Present Progressive

d) Wenn wir eine feste Verabredung oder einen festen Plan für die nahe Zukunft haben verwenden wir:

- ☐ Simple Present
- ☐ Present Progressive

e) Welche Zeitform verwendest du mit folgenden Signalwörtern: ***Look!, now?***

- ☐ Simple Present
- ☐ Present Progressive

f) Wenn wir eine Geschichte erzählen und die Handlungen finden nacheinander statt verwenden wir:

- ☐ Simple Present
- ☐ Present Progressive

oder:
www.schuelerhilfe.de/gute-noten
CODE 8196

bearbeitet am | zu erreichende Punktzahl: 18 | erreichte Punktzahl des Schülers

➡ Ab 14 erreichten Punkten kannst du zum nächsten Test übergehen.

Test 79 Simple Past oder Past Progressive

Schwierigkeitsgrad

A 1 **Unterstreiche die unterschiedlichen Zeiten. *Simple Past* in schwarz und *Past Progressive* in grün.** 7

a) I was preparing dinner when Sam arrived.

b) They were discussing when the teacher came in.

c) I was sleeping when the telephone rang.

d) I arrived while the teacher was speaking.

e) She was reading a book when it started raining.

f) First I had breakfast, and then I read a book.

g) She was going to school when they met.

A 2 **Welcher Satz benutzt die richtige Zeitform des Verbs? Kreuze an.** 6

a) ☐ She was playing guitar when he arrived.
☐ She was playing guitar when he was arriving.

b) ☐ While he was waiting, she came in.
☐ While he waited, she was coming in.

c) ☐ Sam had a shower when the baby started crying.
☐ Sam was having a shower when the baby started crying.

d) ☐ First I visited my grandmother, then I went to school.
☐ First I visited my grandmother, then I was going to school.

e) ☐ She was driving when the accident happened.
☐ She was driving when the accident happen.

f) ☐ He was not listening when I was starting the conversation.
☐ He was not listening when I started the conversation.

A 3 **Setze das Verb in der richtigen Zeitform in die Lücke ein.** 3

a) Yesterday I .... *(come)* home from school while my sister .... *(play)* in the garden.

b) I already .... *(do)* my homework and .... *(help)* my grandmother in her garden.

c) I .... *(run)* late for school when the accident .... *(happen)*.

oder:
www.schuelerhilfe.de/gute-noten
CODE 8518

bearbeitet am | zu erreichende Punktzahl: 16 | erreichte Punktzahl des Schülers

➨ Ab 13 erreichten Punkten kannst du zum nächsten Test übergehen.

Test 80 Simple Past oder Past Progressive

Schwierigkeitsgrad

A1 Schreibe das Verb in der richtigen Zeitform in die Lücke. 22

a) They .... football when their mother arrived. *(to play)*

b) I .... my friend last week. *(to visit)*

c) She .... *(to come in)*, ... *(to sit down)* and .... *(to drink)* a coffee.

d) I .... *(to have)* dinner when Tom .... *(to visit)* me.

e) I .... *(to watch)* TV when the phone rang.

f) Sue .... *(to read)* a book when it .... *(to start)* to rain.

g) We .... *(to dance)* when the music .... *(to stop)*.

h) She .... *(to listen)* to the radio when the postman arrived.

i) Anja .... *(to play)* guitar when Tom .... *(to start)* singing.

j) I .... *(to do)* homework at 10 o'clock last night.

k) I .... *(to go)* to school when I .... *(to meet)* my friend.

l) They .... *(to talk)* when the doors .... *(to open)*.

m) They .... *(to sleep)* when Anna .... *(to come back)*.

A2 Lies dir die Sätze durch und kennzeichne die richtigen Sätze mit einem *x*. 6

a)
- ☐ She woke up, was getting dressed and made coffee.
- ☐ She was waking up, got dressed and was making coffee.
- ☐ She woke up, got dressed and made coffee.

b)
- ☐ They talked when he came in.
- ☐ They were talking when he came in.
- ☐ They was talking when he came in.

c)
- ☐ She was standing outside when he was arriving.
- ☐ She stood outside when he arrived.
- ☐ She was standing outside when he arrived.

d)
- ☐ He was writing a letter when the lights went off.
- ☐ He was writing a letter when the lights were going off.
- ☐ He wrote a letter when the lights go off.

e)
- ☐ She was learning when her brother started playing his guitar.
- ☐ She learned when her brother started to play his guitar.
- ☐ She was learning when her brother was starting to play his guitar.

f)
- ☐ The teacher was explaining the homework when the girl interrupted him.
- ☐ The teacher were explaining the homework when the girl interrupted him.
- ☐ The teacher explained the homework when the girl interrupted him.

oder:
www.schuelerhilfe.de/gute-noten
CODE 8518

bearbeitet am | zu erreichende Punktzahl: 19 | erreichte Punktzahl des Schülers

➡ Ab 15 erreichten Punkten kannst du zum nächsten Test übergehen.

Test 81 Simple Past oder Past Progressive

Schwierigkeitsgrad

A1 **Fülle den Lückentext mit Hilfe der Verben aus. Achte dabei auf die Verwendung der richtigen Zeitform.** 12

shine ▪ tumble ▪ text ▪ drive ▪ listen ▪ come ▪ run ▪ feel ▪ go ▪ hear ▪ turn ▪ see

He .... his van along a winding road when he .... out of fuel.
He .... someone in the fresh air and even if the sun ....
he .... quite cold, so he .... back to the van.
As he .... to some music in the radio, he .... a terrible noise as if
something .... down the steep slopes. He .... the radio off when
he .... the disaster: a huge mass of mud .... towards his car.

A2 **Kreuze an, welche Frage oder Verneinung richtig ist.** 4

a)
- ☐ Were you smoking a cigarette when you started to cough?
- ☐ Did you smoked a cigarette when you started to cough?
- ☐ Did you smoke a cigarette when you started to cough?

b)
- ☐ Didn't Sandra was knitting on the sofa at 10 o'clock in the morning.
- ☐ Sandra wasn't knitting on the sofa at 10 o'clock in the morning.
- ☐ Sandra didn't knitting on the sofa at 10 o'clock in the morning.

c)
- ☐ Anton wasn't dancing when I arrived.
- ☐ Anton didn't dance when I arrived.
- ☐ Anton wasn't dancing when I was arriving.

d)
- ☐ Did the dog was catching the cat?
- ☐ Did the dog catch the cat?
- ☐ Was the dog catched the cat?

A3 **Fülle die Lücken mit Hilfe der richtigen Zeitform der Verben aus.** 4

a) Rebecca .... *(go)* and .... *(buy)* herself some ice cream.

b) Ben .... *(tell)* his friend something when a big friendly dog .... *(run)* towards the friends.

c) I .... *(watch)* TV while my mother .... *(make)* dinner.

d) It .... *(rain)* when they .... *(leave)* the house.

oder:
www.schuelerhilfe.de
/gute-noten
CODE 8518

bearbeitet am .... zu erreichende Punktzahl: 20 erreichte Punktzahl des Schülers ....

➡ Ab 16 erreichten Punkten kannst du zum nächsten Test übergehen.

Test 82 *will*-Future oder *going-to*-Future

Schwierigkeitsgrad

A1 Wann benutzt du das *will-future* und wann *going-to?* 6
Ordne die Beschreibungen den Zeiten zu.

- logische Schlussfolgerung
- Vermutungen
- spontane Entscheidungen
- Absicht im Moment des Sprechens bereits vorhanden
- Künftiges Geschehen, das nicht beeinflussbar ist
- Keine spontane Entscheidung

Will-Future	Going-to-Future

A2 Wähle die richtige Antwort aus. 10

a) ☐ Wait a minute. I'll help you.
☐ Wait a minute. I'm going to help you.

b) ☐ Tom will be 15 next Monday.
☐ Tom is going to be 15 next Monday.

c) ☐ Look outside! It will be rain.
☐ Look outside! It is going to rain.

d) ☐ I think she will marry him.
☐ I think she is going to marry him.

e) ☐ I will visit you tomorrow.
☐ I'm going to visit you tomorrow.

f) ☐ We will go to Spain next year.
☐ We are going to go to Spain next year.

g) ☐ I think the train will arrive at 9 o'clock.
☐ I think the train is going to arrive at 9 o'clock.

h) ☐ Sam came home late. He will be tired tomorrow.
☐ Sam came home late. He is going to be tired tomorrow.

i) ☐ It's cold. The streets will be slippery.
☐ It's cold. The streets are going to be slippery.

j) ☐ I think they will close at 8 o'clock.
☐ I think they are going to close at 8 o'clock.

oder:
www.schuelerhilfe.de/gute-noten
CODE 6563

bearbeitet am ____ zu erreichende Punktzahl: 16 erreichte Punktzahl des Schülers ____

➡ Ab 13 erreichten Punkten kannst du zum nächsten Test übergehen.

Test 83 *will*-Future oder *going-to*-Future

Schwierigkeitsgrad

A1 Setze die Sätze in die richtige Zukunftsform. Nutze die Verben in den Klammern. 14

a) I .... my homework in the evening. *(to do)*

b) I think we .... at 6 o'clock. *(to meet)*

c) It .... tomorrow. *(to rain)*

d) You know what? I .... with you. *(to go)*

e) We .... my grandmother on Sunday. *(to visit)*

f) In 2019 more people .... the zoo. *(to visit)*

g) They .... in the afternoon. *(to meet)*

h) I .... at 5 o'clock. *(to leave)*

i) I think my mother .... angry. *(to be)*

j) She .... this dress. *(to like)*

k) Wait! I .... you. *(to help)*

l) Tim .... 18 next Monday. *(to be)*

m) I .... a dinner party this evening. *(to give)*

n) She sneezes. She .... ill tomorrow. *(to be)*

A2 Bilde Sätze mit den angegebenen Wörtern. Setze die Verben in die richtige Zeit. 8
Nutze *will-future* oder *going-to-future*.

a) I • think • to the cinema • go • they

....

b) I • her • at • 8 o'clock • meet

....

c) Meet • tomorrow • we • mother • my

....

d) She • maybe • the • win • match

....

e) Hope • I • pass • test • the • I

....

f) Party • we • have • week • next

....

g) I • Berlin • go • on • Monday

....

h) Think • they • I • be • friends

....

oder:
www.schuelerhilfe.de
/gute-noten
CODE 6563

bearbeitet am | zu erreichende Punktzahl: 22 | erreichte Punktzahl des Schülers

➨ Ab 18 erreichten Punkten kannst du zum nächsten Test übergehen.

Test 84 *will*-Future oder *going-to*-Future

Schwierigkeitsgrad

A 1 Übersetze ins Englische. Nutze *will-future* oder *going-to-future*. 8

a) Ich denke, sie werden sich mögen.

b) Morgen werde ich Fußball spielen.

c) Es regnet. Draußen wird es später nass sein.

d) Warte! Ich fahre mit dir.

e) Ich werde um 8 Uhr gehen.

f) Ich hoffe, der Test wird einfach.

g) Wir gehen morgen Abend ins Kino.

h) Ich werde meine Oma am Sonntag besuchen.

A 2 Beantworte die Fragen, indem du den Vorschlag in Klammern nutzt. Verwende das *will-* oder *going-to-future*. 5

a) What are your plans for the weekend? *(am Samstag Freunde treffen)*

b) When is she arriving? *(3 Stunden)*

c) Excuse me, can you help me? *(ja)*

d) What do you think about this idea? *(Idee großartig)*

e) What are you doing later? *(Fußball spielen)*

oder:
www.schuelerhilfe.de
/gute-noten
CODE 6563

bearbeitet am | zu erreichende Punktzahl: 13 | erreichte Punktzahl des Schülers

➨ Ab 10 erreichten Punkten kannst du zum nächsten Test übergehen.

LERNEINHEIT 8

Die Verben

Test 85 Die modalen Hilfsverben *can* und *can't*

Schwierigkeitsgrad

A1 Ergänze mit *can* oder *can't*. (+) steht für Aussagen und (–) für Verneinungen. 5

a) (+) I ………… swim.

b) (–) I ………… draw.

c) (+) You ………… cook.

d) (–) He ………… walk.

e) (+) We ………… jump.

A2 Beantworte die folgenden Fragen in vollständigen Sätzen. Antworte jeweils mit *can* und *can't*. 10

a) Can you read? …………

b) Can he speak? …………

c) Can she write? …………

d) Can you climb trees? …………

e) Can he play football? …………

A3 Ergänze mit *can* oder *can't*. 5

a) Cats ………… drive.

b) Planes ………… fly.

c) Bears ………… climb trees.

d) Babies ………… write.

e) Monkeys ………… ride bikes.

oder:
www.schuelerhilfe.de
/gute-noten
CODE 9922

bearbeitet am | zu erreichende Punktzahl: 20 | erreichte Punktzahl des Schülers

➨ Ab 16 erreichten Punkten kannst du zum nächsten Test übergehen.

Test 86 Die modalen Hilfsverben *can* und *can't*

Schwierigkeitsgrad

A 1 Ergänze mit *can* oder *can't*. 5

a) Birds .... read books.

b) Dolphins .... swim.

c) A man .... lift a whale.

d) Dogs .... run.

e) Cars .... speak.

A 2 Ergänze mit *can* oder *can't*. 5

a) He .... play tennis very well,
but he .... play soccer: he's not good at soccer.

b) This cake is delicious:
you .... cook very well.

c) Dad, ... I go out tonight?
No, you ....

A 3 Antworte mit *can* oder *can't*. 9

a) Can you play rugby?
No I ...., but I .... play tennis.

b) Can Mr. Smith teach mathematics?
No, ..., but .... teach English.

c) Can you put together computers?
No, ..., but .... put together toys.

d) Can these TV repairmen fix television sets?
Yes, ...

e) Can Tom speak Spanish?
No, ..., but .... speak Italian.

oder:
www.schuelerhilfe.de
/gute-noten
CODE 9922

bearbeitet am | zu erreichende Punktzahl: 19 | erreichte Punktzahl des Schülers

➨ Ab 15 erreichten Punkten kannst du zum nächsten Test übergehen.

Test 87 Die modalen Hilfsverben *can* und *can't*

Schwierigkeitsgrad

A 1 **Ergänze mit *can* oder *can't*.** 5

a) She .... draw good pictures. She is a great painter.

b) Peter always runs marathons. Peter .... run faster than John.

c) .... you drive a car?

d) You .... come to our house if you want.

e) You .... go in there without a ticket.

A 2 **Bilde die Fragen und die passenden Kurzantworten.** 10

a) some fish / walk? *(yes)*

....

b) Peter / swim? *(no)*

....

c) Oliver / ride a bicycle? *(yes)*

....

d) you / speak Chinese? *(no)*

....

e) you / play the guitar? *(yes)*

....

A 3 **Setze *can* oder *can't* ein.** 7

a) I .... speak Spanish. I picked it up while I was in Spain.

b) I .... come to the party. I am really busy.

c) We .... hear you. The music is too loud.

d) Where are my keys? I .... find them.

e) I .... believe it. We won two million dollars.

f) We .... meet tomorrow if you want.

g) .... you make me a cup of tea, please?

oder:
www.schuelerhilfe.de/gute-noten
CODE 9922

bearbeitet am | zu erreichende Punktzahl: 22 | erreichte Punktzahl des Schülers

➨ Ab 18 erreichten Punkten kannst du zum nächsten Test übergehen.

Test 88 Die modalen Hilfsverben *must* und *needn't*

Schwierigkeitsgrad

A1 Beschreibe die Bilder, indem du das richtige modale Hilfsverb unterstreichst/markierst. 3

a) 

People in this area *must / need / mustn't / needn't* smoke.

b) 

Somebody *must / need / mustn't / needn't* wash the clothes.

c) 

Betty *must / need / mustn't / needn't* work because she is on vacation.

A2 Schreibe den Folgesatz mit Hilfe der Wörter, die in den Klammern stehen und wähle entweder *must* oder *needn't*. 7

a) Sue can't ride her bike. *(repair the wheel)*

She ....

b) We already have enough cake. *(buy more cake)*

We ....

c) Tim is very ill. *(write the test)*

He ....

d) I can't put on my old t-shirt. *(buy a new t-shirt)*

I ....

e) You can't listen to music now. *(do your homework)*

You ....

f) The Smiths are here now. *(call them)*

You ....

g) The kids can't play football. *(play in the house)*

They ....

bearbeitet am | zu erreichende Punktzahl: 10 | erreichte Punktzahl des Schülers

➨ Ab 8 erreichten Punkten kannst du zum nächsten Test übergehen.

Test 89 Die modalen Hilfsverben *must* und *needn't*

Schwierigkeitsgrad

A1 **Entscheide bei jedem Satz, ob eine Pflicht, Notwendigkeit oder Freiwilligkeit ausgedrückt wird und verbinde die passende Aussage/Frage mit der passenden Nummer.** 4

a) Ben mustn't play soccer tomorrow because he did not do his duties in the house.

b) I needn't talk to my sister that soon because she is on vacation with her friend.

c) Mom says the kids must learn harder for school so their grades get better.

d) Do you really need to go to that football game?

1) Drückt aus, dass die Person eine Wahl hat.

2) Drückt eine Notwendigkeit aus.

3) Drückt aus, dass die Person keine Wahl hat.

4) Betont, dass die Person sich vermutlich selber dazu verpflichtet.

A2 **Unterstreiche das richtige modale Hilsverb.** 10

a) I *mustn't / needn't* take my jacket. It won't be cold.

b) I *mustn't / needn't* cross this bridge. It's closed.

c) We *mustn't / needn't* be late. The plane will leave in one hour.

d) We *mustn't / needn't* hurry. We have enough time.

e) One *mustn't / needn't* smoke in here. It is not allowed.

f) We have enough cash. We *mustn't / needn't* get more money.

g) You *mustn't / needn't* come to the party if you don't want to.

h) They *mustn't / needn't* mow the lawn, they have a gardener.

i) You *mustn't / needn't* tell this story to anyone else. I trust you.

j) The students *mustn't / needn't* forget their permission slip for the field trip.

A3 **Fülle die Lücken mit dem richtigen modalen Hilfsverb.** 6

a) Joachim .... go to work today. It's his free day.

b) Jessica .... practice the vocabulary for the English test tomorrow.

c) You .... go to the party because you are ill.

d) Tim and Franziska .... drink alcohol. They aren't 18 years old.

e) We .... hurry up. Otherwise we will miss our plane.

f) My parents .... buy food today. They already bought it yesterday.

oder:
www.schuelerhilfe.de/gute-noten
CODE 5656

bearbeitet am | zu erreichende Punktzahl: 20 | erreichte Punktzahl des Schülers

➡ Ab 16 erreichten Punkten kannst du zum nächsten Test übergehen.

Test 90 Die modalen Hilfsverben *must* und *needn't*

Schwierigkeitsgrad ■■■

A1 Ergänze die Lücken im Text und wähle dabei aus den folgenden Wörtern. 6

must ▪ must ▪ mustn't ▪ mustn't ▪ needn't ▪ needn't

a) You .... do your homework.

b) I .... watch TV because I did not tidy up my room.

c) Today our parents .... wash the dishes on their own because we will help them.

d) Next week grandpa .... see the doctor.

e) David .... swim on his own because he is only two years old.

f) I .... take the bus because my mum brings me by car.

A1 Vervollständige den Lückentext mit 6

must ▪ needn't ▪ mustn't

und der richtigen Verbform

open ▪ go ▪ go ▪ write ▪ hurry ▪ walk ▪ forget

a) We've got lots of time to catch the bus, so we ....

b) When you go camping you .... to take warm clothes with you.

c) British children .... to school in the morning and in the afternoon, but they .... on Saturdays.

d) We've got a lot of homework today, we .... a report about our holidays.

e) Andy .... home because his mother always fetches him in the car.

f) You .... the door of a train before the train stops.

A2 Fülle die Lücken im Text. 7

It's the birthday of Ben's mother tomorrow. Like always Ben still .... prepare a lot of things. He .... bake a cake because his grandma does this every year. But he doesn't have any idea for a gift yet, so he really .... to ask his dad for help with that. Once he has finally decided what to give her, he .... take the bus to the city and buy it. So he .... forget his bus ticket from school. Normally he .... buy one, but if he forgets it, he ....

bearbeitet am | zu erreichende Punktzahl: 19 | erreichte Punktzahl des Schülers

➨ Ab 15 erreichten Punkten kannst du zum nächsten Test übergehen.

Test 91 Die modalen Hilfsverben *may* und *might*

Schwierigkeitsgrad

A1 Wähle die richtige Antwort aus. 2

a) Was ist der Unterschied zwischen *may* und *might?*

1) ☐ *May* ist die höflichere Form.

2) ☐ *Might* ist die formellere Form.

3) ☐ *Might* ist die höflichere und auch formellere Form.

4) ☐ *May* ist die formelle, aber nicht die höflichere Form.

b) Wie unterscheiden sich *may* und *might* in der Übersetzung?

1) ☐ *May* klingt etwas unwahrscheinlicher und wird deshalb mit „dürften“ übersetzt; *Might* wird mit „dürfen“ übersetzt.

2) ☐ *Might* klingt etwas unwahrscheinlicher und wird deshalb mit „dürften“ übersetzt; *May* wird mit „dürfen“ übersetzt.

A2 Was sind richtige Verneinungen von *may* und *might?* 2

a) ☐ mayn't

b) ☐ might not

c) ☐ mighn't

d) ☐ not may

e) ☐ may not

f) ☐ mightn't

A3 Fülle die Lücken mit *may* oder *might*. 6

a) Today we have no homework. We .... play football.

b) .... I visit you today?

c) Might I go to the bathroom, please? Yes, you ....

d) My dad .... be on time today, but usually he is 10 minutes late.

e) I .... be at home the whole afternoon, I don't have a lot to do.

f) .... I ask you a question?

bearbeitet am | zu erreichende Punktzahl: 10 | erreichte Punktzahl des Schülers

➨ Ab 8 erreichten Punkten kannst du zum nächsten Test übergehen.

Test 92 Die modalen Hilfsverben *may* und *might*

Schwierigkeitsgrad

A 1 Fülle die Lücken mit den richtigen Formen von *may* und *might*. 9

a) .... Sarah join you to the doctor?

b) I think that my advice .... be very helpful to you.

c) .... I interrupt you? I have an important question.

d) I .... not be able to finish the whole pizza. I'm already full.

e) I .... finish the whole pizza, but I'm already so full.

f) Mr. Thompson, might we leave earlier today? No, you ....

g) May we make a break here? No, we ....

h) It .... rain today, as it did the whole week already.

i) It .... rain today, but the whole week we had sunny weather.

A 2 Schreibe die Sätze so um, dass du die modalen Hilfsverben *may* und *might* verwenden kannst. 4

a) We are not allowed to do our homework with a red pen.

....

b) It is possible that we miss the train, because we are very late.

....

c) However, it is possible that we catch the train, if the train is late as well.

....

d) There are high chances of rain today. It looks very cloudy.

....

A 3 Bilde Kurzantworten mit der richtigen Form von *may* oder *might*. 4

a) Might I open the window, please? (+)

....

b) May I borrow your green pullover today? (–)

....

c) May we buy a chocolate bar from the shop, please? (+)

....

d) We are not ready yet. Might we stay for some minutes longer? (–)

....

bearbeitet am | zu erreichende Punktzahl: 17 | erreichte Punktzahl des Schülers

➨ Ab 14 erreichten Punkten kannst du zum nächsten Test übergehen.

Test 93 Die modalen Hilfsverben *may* und *might*

Schwierigkeitsgrad ■■■

A1 Fülle die Lücken mit *may* oder *might*. 6

a) Where is Harry? – He …………………… be at the library. I saw him there yesterday.

b) Where is Jenny? – I'm not sure but ask Tom. He …………………… know.

c) We …………………… not leave the room before he has finished his presentation.

d) Do you know where my purse is? – I have no idea. You …………………… have left it at the restaurant.

e) Running around in the rain with only wearing a t-shirt is not healthy! You …………………… be sick tomorrow.

f) Right, but I …………………… still be healthy and fit because I have a good immune system.

A2 Bringe die Wörter in die richtige Reihenfolge. Verwende auch *may* und *might*. 4

a) not ▪ walk ▪ we ▪ school ▪ to ▪ today ……………………

b) put ▪ I ▪ my ▪ bag ▪ here ▪ ? ……………………

c) also ▪ I ▪ cake ▪ of ▪ have ▪ piece ▪ a ▪ ? ……………………

d) snow ▪ tomorrow ▪ it ……………………

A3 Übersetze die folgenden Sätze. Verwende dabei die modalen Hilfsverben. 7

a) Dürfte ich bitte das Fenster öffnen?

……………………

b) Darf ich heute dein Buch ausleihen?

……………………

c) Wir könnten auch Tennis spielen.

……………………

d) Jenny könnte auch in ihrem Zimmer sein.

……………………

e) Tom darf heute mit dem Auto zur Schule fahren.

……………………

f) Mama hat heute vielleicht keine Zeit, dir bei den Hausaufgaben zu helfen.

……………………

g) Siehst du die Wolken? Heute Nacht könnte es regnen.

……………………

oder: www.schuelerhilfe.de/gute-noten
CODE 8515

bearbeitet am | zu erreichende Punktzahl: 17 | erreichte Punktzahl des Schülers

➨ Ab 14 erreichten Punkten kannst du zum nächsten Test übergehen.

Test 94 Das Verb *to be*

Schwierigkeitsgrad

A1 **Setze die richtigen Formen von *to be (am, are, is)* in die Lücken ein.** 8

a) Today .... Monday.

b) My parents .... at home.

c) The weather .... nice.

d) I .... 10 years old.

e) My siblings .... twins.

f) We .... at home.

g) My bed .... very comfortable.

h) Do you think I .... a good student?

A2 **Setze die Kurzformen von *to be ('m, 're, 's)* in die Lücken ein.** 8

a) She' .... at school.

b) They' .... in America.

c) I' .... tired.

d) We' .... on holiday.

e) He' .... a good tennis player.

f) She' .... funny.

g) They' .... late.

h) I' .... hungry.

A3 **Kreuze die richtige Form an.** 8

a) Germany ☐ are / ☐ is a beautiful country.

b) The books ☐ am / ☐ are on the table.

c) The flowers ☐ are / ☐ is in the vase.

d) My friend ☐ is / ☐ are always late.

e) My grandma ☐ am / ☐ is very old.

f) I ☐ are / ☐ am at school.

g) The film ☐ is / ☐ are scary.

h) I ☐ is / ☐ am a hero.

oder:
www.schuelerhilfe.de
/gute-noten
CODE 7451

bearbeitet am | zu erreichende Punktzahl: 24 | erreichte Punktzahl des Schülers

➨ Ab 19 erreichten Punkten kannst du zum nächsten Test übergehen.

Test 95 Das Verb *to be*

Schwierigkeitsgrad

A1 Setze die richtigen Wörter ein. 7

it's • she's • he's • they're • we're • you're • I'm

a) Where are my clothes? .... on the chair.

b) How is the weather today? .... rainy.

c) Where is your sister? .... in England.

d) Tom, how are you? .... fine, thank you.

e) Who is Mister Schmidt? .... our new neighbour.

f) Are you and your brother twins? No, ... only siblings.

g) Am I too late, grandpa? Yes, ... too late.

A2 Entscheide dich zwischen den Formen und kreuze die richtige an. 6

a) I ☐ 'm not / ☐ aren't good at maths.

b) We ☐ aren't / ☐ isn't in Ireland right now.

c) I ☐ isn't / ☐ 'm not 20 years old.

d) She ☐ aren't / ☐ isn't good at sports.

e) He ☐ isn't / ☐ 'm not on holiday.

f) They ☐ aren't / ☐ isn't married.

A3 Bilde mit den vorgegebenen Satzteilen Fragen. 6

a) 15 years • is • old • he

....

b) are • in the • you • garden

....

c) parents • your • are • German

....

d) warm • it • is • today

....

e) Sophia • your • is • friend

....

f) dog • is • black • your

....

oder: www.schuelerhilfe.de /gute-noten
CODE 7451

bearbeitet am | zu erreichende Punktzahl: 19 | erreichte Punktzahl des Schülers

➡ Ab 15 erreichten Punkten kannst du zum nächsten Test übergehen.

Test 96 Das Verb *to be*

Schwierigkeitsgrad ■■■

A1 Ergänze die richtigen Formen von *to be* in dem Lückentext. 13

am ▪ am ▪ am ▪ am ▪ am ▪ am ▪ is ▪ is ▪ is ▪ is ▪ is ▪ are ▪ are

a) Hello, I .... Maja, what is your name? – Hi, I .... Pia and I .... from Germany.

b) Oh, I like Germany. It .... a beautiful country. – Yes, it ....

c) Where .... you from?

d) I .... from Sweden. – Sweden? Where .... it? – It .... in the north of Europe.

e) And what .... you doing here in London? – I .... on holiday, and you?

f) I .... here because my grandparents have a house in London. – That's very cool.

g) Yes, it ....

A2 Setze die richtigen Vergangenheitsformen *(was, were)* von *to be* ein. 5

a) Yesterday my best friend .... ill. I .... sad because I couldn't see her.

b) My family .... at home the whole day. I .... in the city.

c) Together we .... at a restaurant.

A3 Übersetze die folgenden Sätze ins Englische. 5

a) Hallo, wie geht es dir?

....

b) Mir geht es gut.

....

c) Ich komme aus Deutschland.

....

d) Ich war gestern in der Schule.

....

e) Wir waren auf einem Konzert.

....

bearbeitet am ______ zu erreichende Punktzahl: 23 erreichte Punktzahl des Schülers ______

➨ Ab 18 erreichten Punkten kannst du zum nächsten Test übergehen.

Test 97 Der Imperativ

Schwierigkeitsgrad

A1 Vervollständige den Text indem du die richtigen Lösungen in die Lücken einträgst. 10

Befehlsform • Personenzahl • let is • Grundform des Verbes • Aufforderungen, Warnungen, Bitten • Hilfsverb • please • Aufforderungssätze • let us • Verneinung

a) Mit der .... *(Imperativ)* können Befehle, ... und Einladungen ausgedrückt werden.

b) Der Imperativ wird mit der .... ohne „to“ gebildet.

c) In Aufforderungssätzen besitzt das Verb stets die gleiche Form und richtet sich nicht nach der ....

d) Die .... wird mit dem .... „don't“ gebildet.

e) Das Wort „............“ wird zusätzlich verwendet, damit der Imperativ – zum Beispiel bei einer Bitte – nicht unhöflich klingt.

f) Wird der Sprecher mit einbezogen, werden die .... mit „let us / let's“ gebildet.

g) Beachte: „let's“ ist die Kurzform für ...., nicht ....

A2 Verbinde die englischen Aufforderungen mit ihren deutschen Übersetzungen. 10

a) Call me when you are home.	Gib mir bitte mehr Zeit.
b) Don't jump in there!	Hör mir zu/ Hör auf mich!
c) Please pass me the butter.	Sei leise.
d) Let us go inside.	Hör nicht auf ihn!
e) Let's not attract their attention.	Schließe bitte das Fenster.
f) Please shut the window.	Lasst uns nicht ihre Aufmerksamkeit auf uns ziehen.
g) Don't listen to him!	Lasst uns hineingehen.
h) Be quiet.	Reiche mir bitte die Butter.
i) Listen to me!	Spring da nicht hinein!
j) Please give me more time.	Ruf mich an, wenn du zu Hause bist.

bearbeitet am ______ zu erreichende Punktzahl: 20 erreichte Punktzahl des Schülers ______

➡ Ab 16 erreichten Punkten kannst du zum nächsten Test übergehen.

Test 98 Der Imperativ

Schwierigkeitsgrad

A1 Wandle die Sätze in die Befehlsform um. 9

a) He opens the window.

....

b) He cleans his room.

....

c) They eat their sandwiches.

....

d) They are helping their mother.

....

e) They are doing their homework.

....

f) She washes her car.

....

g) He draws a picture for his dad.

....

h) They are getting married.

....

i) It is being done.

....

A2 Forme die Sätze um, indem du den verneinten Imperativ verwendest. 7

a) He puts on the t-shirt. ➨ ....

b) They drink alcohol. ➨ ....

c) We play loud music. ➨ ....

d) I walk on the road. ➨ ....

e) They get lost. ➨ ....

f) He does something bad. ➨ ....

g) She walks away. ➨ ....

oder:
www.schuelerhilfe.de
/gute-noten
CODE 1329

bearbeitet am   **zu erreichende Punktzahl: 16**   **erreichte Punktzahl des Schülers**

➨ Ab 13 erreichten Punkten kannst du zum nächsten Test übergehen.

Test 99 Der Imperativ

Schwierigkeitsgrad

A1 **Bilde eine Forderung *(demand)* oder einen Vorschlag *(suggestion)* im Imperativ, der zur Situation passt.** 7

a) What should we do tomorrow? Go to the beach or something else? *(suggestion)*

....

b) Hendrik and Lisa are doing groceries for dinner. Lisa wants to eat pizza. *(suggestion)*

....

c) The teacher wants to explain the exercise, but the pupils aren't listening. *(demand)*

....

d) The kids are playing inside. One girl wants them all to go outside. *(suggestion)*

....

e) The bell rings and Sam wants Peter to open the door because she is busy. *(demand)*

....

f) A boy and his father are playing in the sandbox. The boy wants his father to eat his sand cake. *(demand)*

....

g) A boy and his father are playing in the sandbox. The boy wants to eat his sand cake together with his father. *(suggestion)*

....

A2 **Fülle die Lücken mit dem Imperativ. Benutze dafür den Infinitiv in den Klammern.** 8

a) .... *(to join)* us! We want to go to the beach.

b) .... *(to not look)*! It's a surprise!

c) I want to be alone. .... *(to go)* away.

d) I am very sad. .... *(to not lie)* to me ever again.

e) I can't talk right now. .... *(to call)* me later.

f) Please .... *(to turn)* down the music. I have a bad headache.

g) .... *(to bring)* me the water, please.

h) .... *(to not play)* with that! It's very sharp and dangerous.

bearbeitet am | zu erreichende Punktzahl: 15 | erreichte Punktzahl des Schülers

➨ Ab 12 erreichten Punkten kannst du zum nächsten Test übergehen.

LERNEINHEIT 9

Die Pronomen

Test 100 Die Personalpronomen: Subjekt- und Objektform

Schwierigkeitsgrad

A1 **Setze die Personalpronomen in die Lücken ein** ***(I, you, he, she, it, we, you, they).*** 8

a) Hey Jenny, can .... help me?

b) Hey John, are .... ready?

c) This is Sarah. .... is five years old.

d) My dad isn't at home. .... is working.

e) Where is Lukas? .... is at school.

f) .... am very tired.

g) Here are my new books. .... are very good.

h) My mother and I, ... often talk about our pets.

A2 **Verwandle die Wörter in den Klammern in Objektpronomen** ***(me, you, him, her, it, us, you, them)*** **und setze diese ein.** 8

a) My mum is writing a letter to .... *(grandma)*

b) Open .... please. *(the door)*

c) The bananas are for .... *(Klaus)*

d) I don't know .... *(the restaurant)*

e) The teacher always gives .... exercises. *(the students)*

f) There's a horse. Can you see .... ? *(the horse)*

g) I am going to the playground. Are you coming with .... ? *(I)*

h) There are Robin and Mark. Say hello to .... *(Robin and Mark)*

A3 **Setze das richtige Pronomen ein:** ***He – We – You – She – They*** 5

a) Have .... got your mobile phone, Svea?

b) .... is from Cologne. *(Lisa)*

c) .... is thinking about her. *(Max)*

d) .... are eating. *(Me and my family)*

e) .... are in the garden. *(the trees)*

oder:
www.schuelerhilfe.de
/gute-noten
CODE 1596

bearbeitet am | zu erreichende Punktzahl: 21 | erreichte Punktzahl des Schülers

➡ Ab 17 erreichten Punkten kannst du zum nächsten Test übergehen.

Test 101 Die Personalpronomen: Subjekt- und Objektform

Schwierigkeitsgrad

A1 Bilde zwei englische Sätze und verwende im zweiten Satz die Personalpronomen. 5

a) Die Johnsons ▪ haben ▪ einen Hund – sie ▪ füttern ▪ ihn ▪ jeden Tag

....

....

b) Lisa ▪ hat ▪ Stifte – sie ▪ benutzt ▪ sie oft

....

....

c) Lars ▪ hat ▪ ein ▪ neues ▪ Auto – er ▪ fährt ▪ es ▪ jeden ▪ Tag

....

....

d) Mama ▪ sieht ▪ eine ▪ alte ▪ Frau – Sie ▪ will ▪ ihr ▪ helfen

....

....

e) Sandra ▪ mag ▪ Blumen – Sie ▪ hat ▪ fünf ▪ davon

....

....

A2 Setze die richtigen Personalpronomen in die Lücken ein. 16

a) Tina has got a new house. .... cleans .... every day.

b) Max und Moritz are at the supermarket. .... buy some fruit.

c) Jenny said: .... love you!

d) Did you hear about our new dog? – We got .... yesterday.

e) .... *(Tom)* is clever.

f) .... *(Pia)* has no idea.

g) .... *(My family and I)* like to eat pizza.

h) Where is the book? I can't find ....

i) .... *(Leslie)* can't come to .... *(Nick's)* party because .... is working.

j) .... *(you and I)* could go to the cinema. What do .... think?

k) Sina, Max and I are so happy, because .... got tickets for the football match.

l) Please, can you help Alexander? .... really needs your help.

oder: www.schuelerhilfe.de/gute-noten
CODE 1596

bearbeitet am | zu erreichende Punktzahl: 21 | erreichte Punktzahl des Schülers

➡ Ab 17 erreichten Punkten kannst du zum nächsten Test übergehen.

Test 102 Die Personalpronomen: Subjekt- und Objektform

Schwierigkeitsgrad

A1 **Finde die falschen Personalpronomen und schreibe die richtigen unten auf.** 3

Today is Lisa's birthday. The family will come to visit his. Lisa is very nervous. He has to prepare lots of things. At the moment, she's baking a cake. His mother is decorating the living room.

a) ....

b) ....

c) ....

A2 **Vervollständige die Sätze mit dem richtigen Personalpronomen.** 6

a) *(Bob and I)* The teacher gave a worksheet to ....

b) *(My parents)* I couldn't wait to show the pictures to ....

c) *(Nico)* Carina likes to go to the restaurant with ....

d) *(Berlin)* .... is the capital city of Germany.

e) I go to work with *(Lena)* .... every day.

f) Marcel wears *(the baseball cap)* .... all the time.

A3 **Finde das Objektpronomen in jedem Satz und schreibe es heraus.** 6

a) I am going to school, so I will take her with me. ....

b) Make sure that they like it. ....

c) Do you really love him? ....

d) She always goes to the supermarket with us. ....

e) They are talking about it. ....

f) Listen to me, please. ....

oder:
www.schuelerhilfe.de
/gute-noten
CODE 1596

bearbeitet am | zu erreichende Punktzahl: 15 | erreichte Punktzahl des Schülers

Ab 12 erreichten Punkten kannst du zum nächsten Test übergehen.

Test 103 Die Possessivpronomen

Schwierigkeitsgrad

A1 Setze das passende Possessivpronomen ein. 9

a) This car is .... *(meins)*

b) This bike is .... *(deins)*

c) This flower is .... *(Annas)*

d) This house is .... *(unsers)*

e) This room is .... *(Marks)*

f) This pizza is .... *(Luisas)*

g) This computer is .... *(Papas)*

h) This book is .... *(Mamas)*

i) This bag is .... *(meiner)*

A2 Vervollständige den Dialog. 7

a) Hanna: Hello, who is she? Is she .... mother?

Nick: Yes, she is .... mother. She is 33 years old. And who is he? Is he .... father?

Hanna: You're right, he is .... father.

b) Kai: Please call Paul and Mia, I need .... help.

Lina: Ok, I will call them. Do you need .... help, too?

Kai: Yes, I will need .... help.

A3 Entscheide dich für eine der beiden Formen. 5

a) He treats .... *(her / his)* girlfriend like a queen.

b) I buy .... *(my / mine)* clothes there.

c) The children make .... *(they / their)* beds.

d) .... *(mine / my)* grandma likes to cook.

e) Sina bought .... *(her / hers)* new shoes at the mall.

oder:
www.schuelerhilfe.de
/gute-noten
CODE 4491

bearbeitet am | zu erreichende Punktzahl: 21 | erreichte Punktzahl des Schülers

➡ Ab 17 erreichten Punkten kannst du zum nächsten Test übergehen.

Test 104 Die Possessivpronomen

Schwierigkeitsgrad

A1 Entscheide dich für die richtige Antwort. 4

a) This pizza is ... but you can have it.

☐ my ☐ mine ☐ yours

b) This horse is ..., not mine.

☐ yours ☐ my ☐ its

c) This is Michael with ... sister.

☐ her ☐ his ☐ mine

d) She is sitting on ... bed.

☐ his ☐ mine ☐ her

A2 Fülle die Lücken aus. 6

a) The boys have got a car. This is ………………… car.

b) Carla has got a dog. It is ………………… dog.

c) Jonas has got a new room. It is ………………… new room.

d) My parents have got a new bed. This is ………………… bed.

e) I have got a new job and he is ………………… new boss.

f) I have a great English teacher. Mr. Smith is ………………… favourite teacher.

A3 Korrigiere die Fehler in den Sätzen. 4

a) Lukas, is it yours camera? No, this isn't mine camera. I think it's his camera.

…………………………………………………………………………………………

b) Karin, is it your pizza? Yes, it's mine pizza.

…………………………………………………………………………………………

c) Stop, why are you wearing mine clothes Konrad? - Because mye clothes are dirty.

…………………………………………………………………………………………

d) This is my room, please don't sit on mine bed and stop eating yours chocolate.

…………………………………………………………………………………………

bearbeitet am | zu erreichende Punktzahl: 14 | erreichte Punktzahl des Schülers

➡ Ab 11 erreichten Punkten kannst du zum nächsten Test übergehen.

Test 105 Die Possessivpronomen

Schwierigkeitsgrad

A1 Finde die richtige Antwort und markiere sie.

5

a) Excuse me. Have you seen ... sister? I can't find her.

mine • my • hers

b) What do you like to do in ... free time?

yours • ours • your

c) This cat belongs to Mirja. It is ... cat.

you • his • her

d) It's not her mobile phone, it's ... . I bought it yesterday.

mine • my • his

e) My father doesn't like ... new job.

her • his • their

A2 Vervollständige den Dialog.

10

Philip: I would like to see .... new house. Is it possible?

Nina: Of course, you can see .... new house. This is .... kitchen and there is .... living room.

Philip: It looks very nice! Where is .... sister's room?

Nina: .... sister's room is upstairs. I will show you. Look, here is .... room. She got a new bed.

Philip: .... room looks really pretty. Can you show me your room, too?

Nina: Yes, this is .... room. It is the biggest room.

Philip: And where is your parent's room?

Nina: .... room is next to my room.

A3 Vervollständige die Sätze.

4

a) I like .... garden but .... is bigger. *(we / you)*

b) .... dog is young and .... dog is very old. *(I / you)*

c) .... parents live in Austria and .... parents live in Cologne. *(he / she)*

d) .... mobile phone has a better camera than .... *(I / you)*

oder:
www.schuelerhilfe.de
/gute-noten
CODE 4491

bearbeitet am | zu erreichende Punktzahl: 19 | erreichte Punktzahl des Schülers

Ab 15 erreichten Punkten kannst du zum nächsten Test übergehen.

Test 106 Demonstrativpronomen

Schwierigkeitsgrad

A 1 Fülle die Lücken mit *this* oder *these.* (6)

a) .... are my new boots.

b) .... are my parents.

c) .... is my brother.

d) .... is my sister.

e) .... is our dog.

f) .... are our cats.

A 2 Fülle die Lücken mit *that* oder *those.* (6)

a) .... are interesting books.

b) .... is a new supermarket.

c) .... is a green tree.

d) .... are good looking people.

e) .... is a new teacher.

f) .... are new neighbours.

A 3 Vervollständige den Dialog mit *it, this* oder *that.* (7)

a) A: Hello, can I help you?

B: Yes, can I have a look at .... beautiful watch?

A: Of course, you can try .... on.

B: Thank you, ... is great.

A: .... is 100 dollar.

b) C: I'm looking for a new pullover.

D: What about .... one?

C: No, sorry. I don't like the colour. I prefer .... red one, over there. Can I try .... on?

D: Yes, sure.

oder:
www.schuelerhilfe.de/gute-noten
CODE 1726

bearbeitet am | zu erreichende Punktzahl: 19 | erreichte Punktzahl des Schülers

➨ Ab 15 erreichten Punkten kannst du zum nächsten Test übergehen.

Test 107 Demonstrativpronomen

Schwierigkeitsgrad

A 1 **Setze das richtige Pronomen *(this, these, that, those)* ein.** 6

a) I like .... car very much. It's my sister's car.

b) He doesn't like .... place in Cologne.

c) .... are my best friends.

d) .... was my brother on the phone.

e) .... are her parents over there.

f) .... concert was great yesterday.

A 2 **Entscheide dich für das richtige Pronomen.** 6

a) Look, ☐ this / ☐ that jacket is nice.

b) ☐ These / ☐ those guys over there are my friends.

c) ☐ This / ☐ that was a great evening.

d) Please take ☐ this / ☐ that book and put it on your shelf.

e) ☐ Those ... / ☐ these ... pictures over there are for your wall.

f) My tennis racket broke ☐ that / ☐ this week.

A 3 **Was ist auf deiner Straßenseite und was siehst du auf der anderen Seite? Bilde kurze Sätze.** 4

	Your side:	other side:
	Mann	Kinder
a)	Mädchen	Frau
b)	Auto	LKW
c)	Blumen	Baum
d)	Hunde	Katzen

Beispiel

➨ I can see this man and those children.

a) ....

b) ....

c) ....

d) ....

oder:
www.schuelerhilfe.de/gute-noten
CODE 1726

bearbeitet am   zu erreichende Punktzahl: 16   erreichte Punktzahl des Schülers

➨ Ab 13 erreichten Punkten kannst du zum nächsten Test übergehen.

Test 108 Demonstrativpronomen

Schwierigkeitsgrad ■■■

A1 Entscheide dich für eine der Antworten. 5

a) ... was such an interesting lesson.

☐ that ☐ this ☐ such ☐ these

b) Are ... your trainers?

☐ That ☐ those ☐ it ☐ this

c) Please give me one of ... books.

☐ those ☐ such ☐ this ☐ that

d) You'll have to get your own paper. ... is mine.

☐ these ☐ those ☐ it ☐ this

e) ... guys are nice-looking.

☐ these ☐ it ☐ such ☐ this

A2 Entscheide dich für ein Pronomen und ergänze den Satz. 5

a) .... books here are mine.

b) .... supermarket across the street sells delicious fruits.

c) .... children over there are my friends.

d) .... is the day we'll win the football match.

e) I'd like to buy .... teddy bear.

A3 Was ist das Demonstrativpronomen? Schreibe es hinter jeden Satz. 5

a) That is the pullover I would like to buy. ....

b) Would you like some of these? ....

c) This is my favorite picture. ....

d) Those years in America were the best years of my life. ....

e) That car over there is the best one. ....

bearbeitet am | zu erreichende Punktzahl: 15 | erreichte Punktzahl des Schülers

➡ Ab 12 erreichten Punkten kannst du zum nächsten Test übergehen.

Test 109 Die Reflexivpronomen

Schwierigkeitsgrad

A1 Ordne die Reflexivpronomen in die Tabelle ein. 8

himself · myself · itself · yourself · ourselves · themselves · herself · yourselves

Singular	1. Person	I	
	2. Person	you	
	3. Person	he	
		she	
		it	
Plural	1. Person	we	
	2. Person	you	
	3. Person	they	

A2 Sind die folgenden Aussagen zum Thema Reflexivpronomen wahr oder falsch? Kreuze an. 12

		wahr	falsch
a)	Reflexivpronomen werden auch rückbezügliche Fürwörter genannt.	☐	☐
b)	Mit Reflexivpronomen kann betont werden, dass eine Person etwas selbst tut.	☐	☐
c)	Reflexivpronomen können stellvertretend für das Subjekt in einem Satz stehen.	☐	☐
d)	Reflexivpronomen können weggelassen werden.	☐	☐
e)	Im Englischen steht in der Einzahl ***-self*** und in der Mehrzahl ***-selves*** am Ende der Reflexivpronomen.	☐	☐
f)	Reflexivpronomen beziehen sich auf das Subjekt im Satz.	☐	☐
g)	Reflexivpronomen werden verwendet, wenn man betonen möchte, dass jemand etwas ohne fremde Hilfe geschafft hat.	☐	☐
h)	Im Englischen gibt es weniger Verben, die reflexiv verwendet werden, als im Deutschen.	☐	☐
i)	Reflexivpronomen stehen immer direkt hinter dem Subjekt, auf das sie sich beziehen.	☐	☐
j)	Reflexivpronomen werden auch besitzanzeigende Fürwörter genannt.	☐	☐
k)	Reflexivpronomen werden verwendet, wenn Subjekt und Objekt in einem Satz dieselbe Person haben.	☐	☐
l)	Um auszudrücken, dass etwas gegenseitig oder miteinander geschieht, wird statt der Reflexivpronomen ***each other*** verwendet.	☐	☐

bearbeitet am ______ zu erreichende Punktzahl: 20 erreichte Punktzahl des Schülers ______

➨ Ab 16 erreichten Punkten kannst du zum nächsten Test übergehen.

Test 110 Die Reflexivpronomen

Schwierigkeitsgrad

A1 Schreibe alle Reflexivpronomen aus folgenden Sätzen heraus. 6

a) You can do it yourself. ....

b) We enjoyed ourselves yesterday. ....

c) Lisa hurt herself. ....

d) Children, please behave yourselves. ....

e) I would like to introduce myself. ....

f) Mark looks at himself in the mirror. ....

A2 Ordne die folgenden Verben ihrer passenden deutschen Übersetzung zu. 14

a) to behave oneself	**1.** sich fühlen
b) to change	**2.** sich beeilen
c) to concentrate	**3.** sich (hin)setzen
d) to cut oneself	**4.** sich ausdrücken
e) to dry oneself	**5.** sich benehmen
f) to enjoy oneself	**6.** sich schneiden
g) to express oneself	**7.** sich treffen
h) to feel	**8.** sich vorstellen
i) to hurry	**9.** sich amüsieren
j) to hurt oneself	**10.** sich (ver-)ändern
k) to introduce oneself	**11.** sich abtrocknen
l) to meet	**12.** sich konzentieren
m) to remember	**13.** sich verletzen
n) to sit down	**14.** sich erinnern

A3 Welche der englischen Verben aus A1 sind reflexiv? 7

a) ....

b) ....

c) ....

d) ....

e) ....

f) ....

g) ....

bearbeitet am | zu erreichende Punktzahl: 27 | erreichte Punktzahl des Schülers

➡ Ab 21 erreichten Punkten kannst du zum nächsten Test übergehen.

Test 111 Die Reflexivpronomen

Schwierigkeitsgrad ■■■

A1 Hoppla, in den folgenden Sätzen wurden alle Reflexivpronomen vergessen. Ergänze sie. Achtung, es müssen nicht alle Lücken gefüllt werden! 26

a) Let me introduce ..., my name is Mrs. Marshall and I am your new English teacher.

b) I love art. It is a way to express ... .

c) Enjoy ... at the party tonight. I heard they invited a surprise guest.

d) Patrick doesn't want to hurt ..., so he is very careful.

e) Girls, you can be really proud of ... .

f) The president ... talked to the people on the street.

g) He doesn't need our help. He can defend ... .

h) My Mum cut ... while making dinner.

i) Did you eat the whole cake ... ?

j) Mary taught ... to change her car tires.

k) The dirty dishes don't wash ... .

l) The child cannot remember ... the name of the street.

m) He didn't sleep very well last night, so today he feels tired ... .

n) She brought a birthday cake for ... .

o) Children, please behave ... during class.

p) We will move the furniture ... .

q) The candle went out by ... .

r) After taking a shower you have to dry ... .

s) We are talking to ... on the phone.

t) I can't help you any longer, you have to finish your homework ... .

u) He felt very sad ... when she left him.

v) I can open the door ... .

w) She cuts ... her own hair.

x) We fixed our bikes all by ... .

y) The cat licked ... .

z) Sebastian can't see ... in the mirror, because he is a vampire.

bearbeitet am ___ zu erreichende Punktzahl: 26 erreichte Punktzahl des Schülers ___

➡ Ab 21 erreichten Punkten kannst du zum nächsten Test übergehen.

10 LERNEINHEIT

Abschlusstest

Test 112 Abschlusstest – Teil 1 von 3

Der Satzbau

A1 Bei welchen Sätzen ist der Satzbau richtig? Kreuze an. (4)

a)
- ☐ I on Sundays my dog to play take out.
- ☐ On Sundays I take out my dog to play.
- ☐ My dog to play take out I on Sundays.

b)
- ☐ Does it rain in England every day?
- ☐ In England does every day it rain?
- ☐ Rain it does in England every day?

c)
- ☐ Don't they like to ride their old bikes.
- ☐ They don't like to ride their old bikes.
- ☐ Their like to don't ride they old bikes.

d)
- ☐ Not driving we are to the city right now.
- ☐ Are not we now to the city driving right.
- ☐ We are not driving to the city right now.

Der Gebrauch der verschiedenen Zeiten

A2 Vervollständige die Sätze indem du die Verben in den Klammern entweder im *Simple Present* oder im *Present Progressive* einträgst. (6)

a) The team .... *(not play)* in the first football league, but it .... *(win)* every match.

b) I .... *(not watch)* TV because I .... *(do)* my homework at the moment.

c) My teacher .... *(like)* to tell us stories and we always .... *(want)* the story with the wizards.

d) .... *(be)* we .... *(listen)* to the radio and .... *(play)* a game of cards right now?

e) They .... *(read)* one book every week but Susan .... *(read)* two books, because she is such a fast reader.

f) Their kids .... *(not go)* to the party, because they .... *(be)* mean right now.

Test 112 Abschlusstest – Teil 2 von 3

A 3 **Vervollständige die Sätze indem du die Verben entweder im *Simple Past* oder *Past Progressive* einträgst.** 6

a) While I .... *(play)*, the bus .... *(arrive)*.

b) Jonas .... *(become)* sick while he .... *(travel)*.

c) .... you .... *(go)* to school yesterday?

d) .... they .... *(wait)* for her with the movie when she .... *(come)* too late?

e) She .... *(say)* that she .... *(not feel)* happy, so I .... *(talk)* to her.

f) What .... you .... *(do)* when you .... *(hear)* about 9/11?

A 4 **Umkreise die richtige Form des Verbs.** 4

a) I usually ***go / am going / went / were going*** to Judo on Mondays but not yesterday since I ***have / am having / had / was having*** a fever during practice time.

b) My mother ***makes / is making / made / were making*** the best pancakes and last week we ***eat / are eating / ate / were eating*** some while my father ***work / is working / worked / was working***.

c) When I ***come / am coming / came / was coming*** from my vacation last week my little brother ***is / is being / was / was being*** ill.

d) Harry: "What ***do / are doing / did / were doing*** you want Sue?" Sue: "I ***want / am wanting / wanted / were wanting*** to know which route you usually ***take / are taking / took / were taking*** to school."

Die Pronomen

A 5 **Vervollständige die Sätze indem du die richtigen *Personal-* oder *Possessivpronomen* einsetzt.** 6

a) Lisa: "Mr. Müller is .... teacher. .... is always late.

b) Max: "................ am Max and this is .... brother Moritz. .... mother is called Maria and .... are ten years old.

c) There are four dogs running to the river. .... try to cross it. Can you see ....?

d) Joachim: "Hey Frank and Sabine! .... need .... help. Can .... help ....?"

e) Barbara: "Look at .... new game. .... can test ....!"

f) The Laumanns: "Do you know the Hartmann's dog? .... is big but .... is big, too.

Zusatzaufgaben

A 6 **Fill the gaps with the correct form of the verb *to be*.** 5

a) I .... fourteen years old.

b) She .... my sister.

c) Her name .... Tina.

d) .... you ready? Yes, I ....

e) .... he rich? Yes, he ....

Test 112 Abschlusstest – Teil 3 von 3

A7 Fill the gap with the correct *personal* and *possessive pronoun*. Use the pronouns below. 10

yours ▪ they ▪ mine ▪ mine ▪ his ▪ his ▪ you ▪ you ▪ their ▪ my ▪ my ▪ he ▪ her ▪ your ▪ our

a) This is Tom. Sam is .... friend. .... have known each other for five years.

b) Hi, ...name is Linda. What is .... name?

c) This is .... friend .... Lisa. Do .... like .... ?

d) He lives in .... own house.

e) Whose pencil is that? It's ....

f) This is .... son Alex. .... is fifteen years old.

g) Anna and Mona visited .... grandmother.

h) Sam, is this book .... ?

i) I found a chain, now it's ....

j) Can .... help me?

A8 Fill the gaps with the correct form of the verb. Use *Present progressive*. 4

a) They .... *(to laugh)* at the moment.

b) She .... *(to listen)* to the teacher.

c) We .... *(to talk)* about the movie.

d) I .... *(to read)* the newspaper right now.

A9 Fill the gaps with the correct form of the verb. Use *Past Progressive*. 4

a) They .... *(to play)* football in the garden.

b) She .... *(to do)* homework.

c) Anna and Tom .... *(to visited)* their mother.

d) He .... *(to cook)* a soup.

A10 Fill the gap with the correct tense. Use Simple *present* or *present progressive*. 6

a) Look! They .... tennis. *(to play)*

b) Sam usually .... to school at 8 o'clock. *(to go)*

c) Tom always .... a letter, but now he .... an email. *(to write)*

d) She .... to the music at the moment. *(to listen)*

e) They .... the school right now. *(to leave)*

f) The pupils .... a test every Monday. *(to write)*

bearbeitet am | zu erreichende Punktzahl: 65 | erreichte Punktzahl des Schülers

➡ Ab 52 erreichten Punkten hast du den Abschlusstest bestanden.

Test 1 – Das Present Tense: Aussagesätze

A1 **6 Punkte**

a) thinks
b) know
c) buy
d) likes
e) sees
f) eat

A2 **8 Punkte**

a) go
b) likes
c) plays
d) eat
e) loves
f) walks
g) see
h) drive

A3 **5 Punkte**

a) Ollie always sleeps in at the weekend. / At the weekend Ollie always sleeps in.
b) I draw pictures every week. / Every week I draw pictures.
c) My sister often wears my clothes.
d) My brother talks to me every day. / Every day my brother talks to me.
e) My parents often watch TV.

Test 2 – Das Present Tense: Aussagesätze

A1 **4 Punkte**

a) Harry often plays the guitar.
b) We have breakfast every morning.
c) On Saturdays we help our parents and play in the garden. / We help our parents and play in the garden on Saturdays.
d) She learns English at school.

A2 **4 Punkte**

a) + **3)**
b) + **2)**
c) + **2)**
d) + **1)**

A3 **8 Punkte**

a) Ich spiele mit Laura jeden Tag.
b) Sie geht jeden Abend ins Bett.
c) Wir frühstücken jeden Morgen.
d) Ich fahre mittwochs Fahrrad.

Test 3 – Das Present Tense: Aussagesätze

A1 **9 Punkte**

a) She loves her dog.
b) Stefan likes cars.
c) We go to the cinema on Saturday. / On Saturday we go to the cinema.
d) We watch a movie about animals.
e) My mother cooks on Sunday. / On Sunday my mother cooks.
f) We often play a game.
g) You like horses.
h) I brush my teeth every day. / Every day I brush my teeth.
i) Klaus plays on the computer every afternoon. / Every afternoon Klaus plays on the computer.

A2 **5 Punkte**

a) My parents cook every day. / Every day my parents cook.
b) My brother often plays football.
c) I play the piano on Monday and Wednesday. / On Monday and Wednesday I play the piano.
d) I go to school from Monday to Friday. / From Monday to Friday I go to school.
e) My best friend and I meet two times a week. / Two times a week my best friend and I meet.

Test 4 – Das Present Tense: Fragesätze

A1 **8 Punkte**

a) Do
b) Do
c) Does
d) Does
e) Does
f) Do
g) Do
h) Does

A2 **4 Punkte**

a) Yes, he does.
b) No, they don't.
c) No, we don't.
d) Yes, she does.

A3 **4 Punkte**

a) Where
b) When
c) What
d) Why

Test 5 – Das Present Tense: Fragesätze

A1 **8 Punkte**

a) does; work
b) does; leave
c) does; like
d) do; open

A2 **4 Punkte**

a) Can I eat that tomato?
b) Does he eat apples?
c) Do you collect stamps?
d) Do they speak English?

A3 **6 Punkte**

a) where
b) What's/ What is
c) How old are you
d) when
e) What; is
f) why

Test 6 – Das Present Tense: Fragesätze

A1 **2 Punkte**

a) ☒ Do
b) ☐ Have not
c) ☐ Does
d) ☐ Do not
e) ☒ Don't

A2 **6 Punkte**

a) Does Sally teach at your school?
b) Don't you know the answer?
c) When do the Smiths visit London?
d) Doesn't it look like rain?
e) Do the students wait for the bus?
f) Where does aunt Susan live?

A3 **4 Punkte**

a) Do you eat alone?
b) How many chairs do you need?
c) Do you like something to drink?
d) Do you want milk for your coffee?

Test 7 – Das Present Tense: Verneinte Sätze

A1 **4 Punkte**

b); **c)**; **e)**; **f)**

A2 **6 Punkte**

a) don't
b) don't
c) doesn't
d) doesn't
e) doesn't
f) don't

A3 **5 Punkte**

a) My father isn't a police officer.
b) The students don't like Mondays.
c) I can't speak Spanish.
d) He doesn't write a letter.
e) I don't know the headmaster.

Lösungen

Test 8 – Das Present Tense: Verneinte Sätze

A1 **4 Punkte**

a); c); d); e)

A2 **4 Punkte**

a) No, I don't / do not know Mrs. Collins.

b) Why don't you go? / Why do you not go?

c) He isn't/ is not in New York City.

d) Sarah doesn't listen / does not listen to music.

A3 **4 Punkte**

a) she doesn't know

b) she doesn't know

c) we don't know

d) he doesn't know

Test 9 – Das Present Tense: Verneinte Sätze

A1 **4 Punkte**

a) wahr

b) wahr

c) falsch

d) wahr

A2 **5 Punkte**

a) (The) students don't like English lessons on Friday afternoon.

b) The woman at the information desk can't help the tourists.

c) Jason's parents aren't at home.

d) The girl doesn't wait for the bus.

e) Don't throw the ball!

A3 **4 Punkte**

a) Don't look

b) Don't speak

c) Don't open

d) Don't talk

Test 10 – Das Present Progressive: Aussagesätze

A1 **5 Punkte**

a) I am reading a book.

b) We are singing a new song.

c) He is buying a magazine.

d) Sarah is doing her homework.

e) Papa is writing a letter.

A2 **5 Punkte**

a) is working

b) are watching

c) is playing

d) are cleaning

e) is raining

Test 11 – Das Present Progressive: Aussagesätze

A1 **5 Punkte**

a) is reading

b) is watching

c) are playing

d) is cleaning

e) is storming.

A2 **5 Punkte**

a) He is reading the newspaper.

b) We are playing with the ball.

c) They are buying tickets for the cinema.

d) Jane and Jenny are washing the dishes.

e) Mr. Miller is washing his car.

A3 **5 Punkte**

a) Rafael is watching a movie.

b) We are playing a funny game.

c) The dog is barking at the cat.

d) Oliver is feeding his pets.

e) Philipp and Johnny are singing a wonderful song.

Test 12 – Das Present Progressive: Aussagesätze

A1 **6 Punkte**

a) Andrew and my mother are baking muffins.
b) Paul is writing a letter.
c) Alexander is dancing with his wife Angelika.
d) They are taking a shower.
e) I am saving money for a new computer game.
f) He is cutting the grass.

A2 **14 Punkte**

a) is going
b) is wearing; is carrying
c) cycles; is taking; is raining
d) leaves; arrives
e) begins; live; am doing
f) wear; am working; am wearing

Test 13 – Das Present Progressive: Fragesätze

A1 **14 Punkte**

a) Is
b) Are
c) Are
d) Is
e) Are
f) Is
g) Are
h) No, she isn't.
i) No, they aren't.
j) Yes, I am.
k) Yes, she is.
l) Yes, we are. / Yes, you are.
m) No, he isn't.
n) No, I'm not.

A2 **4 Punkte**

a) Is she flying to America?
b) Are you eating pizza?
c) Is he crying?
d) Are they listening to a CD?

Test 14 – Das Present Progressive: Fragesätze

A1 **7 Punkte**

a) Am I reading a book?
b) Are we eating a pizza?
c) Are they looking tired?
d) Is she playing with her teddy?
e) Is he watching a football match?
f) Is my mum taking a shower?
g) Is dad repairing our car?

A2 **6 Punkte**

a) Is my sister riding a horse?
b) Is my brother playing football?
c) Am I going to the cinema?
d) Is mum buying fruits at the supermarket?
e) Are we brushing our teeth in the bathroom?
f) Are we eating spaghetti?

Lösungen

Test 15 – Das Present Progressive: Fragesätze

A1 **7 Punkte**

a) Is your sister searching for a new house?

b) Are you wearing trousers or a skirt today?

c) Is Lisa visiting her boyfriend?

d) Are you talking about important things with your grandparents?

e) Is Otto reading comics or books?

f) Is he taking the car or the bus?

g) Are they eating outside because it's summer?

A2 **16 Punkte**

a) Mr. Smith: Hi, **are** you ready to go to the restaurant?

Mrs. Smith: Yes, I **am.** I **am coming** to your car now. **Are** you **waiting** for me?

Mr. Smith: Oh yes, I **am waiting** for you. You **are looking** great tonight.

b) Our family **is** in the garden today. The sun **is shining** and the children **are having** fun. My mum **is looking** after the flowers and my dad **is reading** the newspapers. My siblings **are playing** badminton. Bello, our dog **is sleeping** in the sun.

c) In the zoo a little fish **is swimming** in the aquarium. A monkey **is climbing** up a tree and another monkey **is playing** with the baby monkey.

Test 16 – Das Present Progressive: Verneinte Sätze

A1 **6 Punkte**

a) aren't
b) isn't
c) isn't
d) aren't
e) isn't
f) 'm not

A2 **8 Punkte**

a) isn't going
b) aren't playing
c) isn't watching
d) 'm not riding
e) aren't buying
f) isn't looking
g) 'm not wearing
h) isn't cooking

A3 **8 Punkte**

a) Mika isn't sleeping.

b) My sister isn't brushing her teeth.

c) Granpa isn't reading the newspaper

d) We aren't drawing a picture.

e) I'm not going to bed.

f) Dad isn't repairing the car.

g) Mum isn't watching a movie.

h) Felix isn't taking a shower.

Test 17 – Das Present Progressive: Verneinte Sätze

A1 **6 Punkte**

a) isn't writing
b) isn't doing
c) 'm not calling
d) isn't playing
e) isn't meeting
f) aren't learning

A2 **6 Punkte**

a) aren't looking
b) aren't helping
c) isn't playing
d) 'm not driving
e) isn't relaxing
f) isn't closing

A3 **6 Punkte**

a) We aren't going home now.

b) They aren't working today.

c) I'm not loving you.

d) My parents aren't watching TV.

e) Kira isn't crying.

f) Tom isn't visiting a restaurant.

Test 18 – Das Present Progressive: Verneinte Sätze

A1 **10 Punkte**

a) My class isn't buying a present for my birthday but I'm not sad about it. We're celebrating my birthday in a restaurant, we are staying at home. My friends are coming but my grandma isn't coming because she's ill.

b) My sister **isn't sitting** on the sofa. She is talking to her boyfriend in the kitchen, but **they're not cooking.** They **are not** hungry.

c) Right now, Ben and Anna are eating breakfast. Anna **isn't drinking** coffee. She prefers tea. Ben **isn't drinking** tea. They are eating cornflakes but they **aren't having** milk.

A2 **6 Punkte**

a) aren't
b) learning
c) isn't
d) seeing
e) aren't
f) visiting

A3 **2 Punkte**

a) She isn't playing computer because she isn't feeling well.

b) They aren't driving their car because dad is repairing it.

Test 19 – Das Past Tense: Das Verb *to be* im Simple Past

A1 **8 Punkte**

a) was
b) were
c) was
d) were
e) were
f) were
g) wasn't
weren't

A2 **5 Punkte**

a) was
b) were
c) were
d) was
e) were

A3 **7 Punkte**

a) Were
b) wasn't
c) weren't
d) Was
e) wasn't
f) Were
g) wasn't

Test 20 – Das Past Tense: Das Verb *to be* im Simple Past

A1 **10 Punkte**

Last August we **were** on holiday in America. It **was** an amazing holiday even though my family **was** in a pretty bad hotel. The rooms **were** not nice and very dirty, but all the people **were** really friendly. The food in the restaurant **was** okay, but the soup **was** cold. And the ice cream **was** melted, too. But I **was** by the ocean every day, and my parents **were** at the beach, too.

A2 **5 Punkte**

a) wasn't
b) weren't
c) wasn't
d) wasn't
e) weren't

A3 **10 Punkte**

a) Was
b) Were
c) Were
d) Was
e) Was
f) Were
g) Was
h) Were
i) Was
j) Was

Test 21 – Das Past Tense: Das Verb *to be* im Simple Past

A1 **8 Punkte**

a) was – was
b) Was – wasn't – was
c) Were – weren't – were
d) wasn't – wasn't – was
e) Was – wasn't – was – were
f) Was – was
g) Were – weren't – were
h) Were – weren't – wasn't

A2 **4 Punkte**

a) Was she there? – Wasn't she there?
b) Were they there?
c) Were we there? – Weren't we there?
d) She was there but they weren't. – She wasn't there but they were.

Test 22 – Das Past Tense: Das Verb *to be* im Simple Past

A1 **9 Punkte**

a) was
b) was
c) was
d) were
e) was
f) was
g) was
h) were
i) was

A2 **4 Punkte**

a) 1)
b) 2)
c) 1)
d) 3)

Test 23 – Das Past Tense: Das Verb *to be* im Simple Past

A1 **5 Punkte**

a) Yes, the clothes store was still open.
b) Sarah and Jenny were responsible for the cakes.
c) No, the bananas weren't on sale at the supermarket.
d) Yes, the show was two hours ago.
e) No, Ben wasn't waiting outside already.

A2 **5 Punkte**

a) wasn't
b) weren't
c) aren't
d) wasn't
e) wasn't

A3 **5 Punkte**

a) wanted to be
b) tried to be
c) hoped to be
d) asked me to be
e) want to be

Test 24 – Das Past Tense: Das Verb *to be* im Simple Past

A1 **4 Punkte**

a) Was the cake sold out already?
b) Who was away with the car tonight?
c) Were the actors welcomed at the red carpet tonight?
d) Do you know where Ben was last weekend?

A2 **6 Punkte**

a) was wearing
b) were laughing
c) was
d) was just asking
e) were
f) was

A3 **3 Punkte**

a) I was praised for being the best piano player.
b) Yesterday, my dad was asked to donate money.
c) The children were at their grandma's las week.

Test 25 – Das Past Tense: Die regelmäßigen Verben

A1 **3 Punkte**

a) ☒ Sally phoned her uncle.
b) ☐ I have been in Canada.
c) ☒ She had an accident.
d) ☐ His friend has a new car.
e) ☒ The tennis players watched the match.

A2 **6 Punkte**

a) walked
b) watched
c) listened
d) danced
e) looked
f) worked

A3 **4 Punkte**

a) I liked ice cream.
b) We moved to Berlin.
c) The cats walked on the wall.
d) Mum cooked a soup.

Test 26 – Das Past Tense: Die regelmäßigen Verben

A1 **4 Punkte**

a) Yes, they wanted popcorn.
b) Yes, he worked on Friday.
c) Yes, we watched the parade.
d) Yes, she liked the book.

A2 **3 Punkte**

a) I played soccer.
b) She asked for help.
c) They repeated the song.

A3 **9 Punkte**

a) opened
b) arrived
c) played
d) talked
e) answered; questioned
f) waited; looked
g) prepared

Test 27 – Das Past Tense: Die regelmäßigen Verben

A1 **3 Punkte**

a) falsch
b) richtig
c) richtig

A2 **5 Punkte**

a) ☐ do
b) ☐ be
c) ☒ walk
d) ☐ write
e) ☒ cry
f) ☒ dance
g) ☐ sleep
h) ☒ want
i) ☐ fly
j) ☒ like

A3 **4 Punkte**

a) The class visited the zoo yesterday. / Yesterday, the class visited the zoo.
b) She used a knife to cut a face into the pumpkin.
c) The girls danced in a cheerleading team 10 years ago. / 10 years ago, the girls danced in a cheerleading team.
d) The students changed their lunch last week. / Last week, the students changed their lunch.

Test 28 – Das Past Tense: Die regelmäßigen Verben

A1 **9 Punkte**

a) planned
b) walked
c) listened
d) talked
e) cooked
f) played
g) learned
h) opened
i) jumped

A2 **12 Punkte**

a) stopped
b) planned
c) baked
d) carried
e) wanted
f) loved
g) asked
h) opened
i) repaired
j) talked
k) enjoyed
l) missed

Test 29 – Das Past Tense: Die regelmäßigen Verben

A1 **8 Punkte**

a) carried
b) visited
c) laughed
d) tried
e) spotted
f) fitted
g) saved
h) hurried

A2 **7 Punkte**

	Simple Present	Simple Past
a)	to suffer	suffered
b)	to control	controlled
c)	to waste	wasted
d)	to close	closed
e)	to swap	swapped
f)	to travel	travelled
g)	to jump	jumped

A3 **7 Punkte**

a; b; c; h; i; k; l

Test 30 – Das Past Tense: Die regelmäßigen Verben

A1 **6 Punkte**

a) I liked the taste of cookies.
b) He worried about his sister Miriam.
c) Maggie followed her heart.
d) My brother Ben reached the school bus.
e) Our aunt Claudia wanted to move to the Netherlands.
f) I travelled to the USA with my boyfriend.

A2 **4 Punkte**

a) I called my mum last week.
b) Yesterday I missed the piano lesson.
c) My father wasn't amused about my test.
d) Yesterday it rained all day.

Test 31 – Das Past Tense: Die unregelmäßigen Verben

A1 **6 Punkte**

a) was/were
b) did
c) had
d) went
e) wrote
f) saw

A2 **6 Punkte**

a) won
b) shut
c) let
d) put
e) hit
f) left

A3 **4 Punkte**

a) The tree stood next to our house.

b) The friends wrote some letters.

c) I took the dog for a walk.

d) The teacher read a magazine.

Test 32 – Das Past Tense: Die unregelmäßigen Verben

A1 **5 Punkte**

a) richtig

b) richtig

c) richtig

d) falsch

e) falsch

A2 **5 Punkte**

a) I did my homework.

b) The dogs were in the park.

c) I had lunch yesterday.

d) Last night, Dr Thomas slept well.

e) My sister bought new jeans.

A3 **6 Punkte**

a) catch

b) think

c) drive

d) rise

e) swim

f) see

Test 33 – Das Past Tense: Die unregelmäßigen Verben

A1 **3 Punkte**

a) flew **b)** saw **c)** could

A2 **4 Punkte**

a) Yes, my class mates understood the exercises.

b) Yes, my brother became a pilot.

c) Yes, the children broke the window.

d) Yes, Anna drew this picture.

A3 **8 Punkte**

a) The pop star wore a nice dress.

b) I wrote letters to my pen friend last summer.

c) Chris threw a/the ball into the neighbour's garden.

d) The coach taught us the rules of football.

Test 34 – Das Past Tense: Die unregelmäßigen Verben

A1 **14 Punkte**

	Infinitiv	Past Simple	Past Participle
a)	to buy	**bought**	bought
b)	**to bring**	brought	brought
c)	**to bite**	bit	bitten
d)	to sing	**sang**	sung
e)	to take	**took**	taken
f)	**to hurt**	hurt	hurt
g)	**to make**	made	made
h)	to sell	**sold**	sold
i)	**to eat**	**ate**	eaten
j)	to sit	**sat**	sat
k)	**to be**	was/were	been
l)	to hit	**hit**	hit
m)	**to freeze**	froze	frozen
n)	to ride	**rode**	ridden

A2 **6 Punkte**

a) richtig

b) to shut – shut – shut

c) to fight – fought – fought

d) to lead – led – led

e) to sleep – slept – slept

f) richtig

Test 35 – Das Past Tense: Die unregelmäßigen Verben

A1 **16 Punkte**

	Übersetzung	Infinitiv	Past Simple	Past Participle
a)	suchen	**to seek**	sought	sought
b)	sinken, untergehen	**to sink**	**sank**	sunk
c)	**zerreißen**	to tear	**tore**	torn
d)	teilen, spalten	to split	**split**	split
e)	ausgeben, verbringen	**to spend**	**spent**	spent
f)	**handeln**	to deal	dealt	dealt
g)	**graben**	to dig	dug	dug
h)	fangen	**to catch**	**caught**	caught

A2 **9 Punkte**

a) caught
b) forgot
c) done
d) drawn
e) ate
f) drank
g) driven
h) forbidden
i) fell

Test 36 – Das Past Tense: Die unregelmäßigen Verben

A1 **18 Punkte**

	Übersetzung	Infinitiv	Past Simple	Past Participle
a)	aufgehen	to rise	rose	risen
b)	lesen	to read	read	read
c)	kennen, wissen	to know	knew	known
d)	bauen	to build	built	built
e)	schütteln	to shake	shook	shaken
f)	werfen	to throw	threw	thrown

A2 **6 Punkte**

a) Last week Maggie and Sue swam in the sea.
b) It took hours to clean the floor.
c) Dirk hasn't been in Australia before.
d) Kai has written hundreds of letters to me.
e) Heinz has sung in a choir for many years.
f) My brother hid my favorite book.

Test 37 – Das Past Tense: Aussagesätze

A1 **5 Punkte**

a) + **2)**
b) + **1)**
c) + **2)**
d) + **3)**
e) + **1)**

A2 **6 Punkte**

a) Yesterday I called Franzi.
b) Yesterday we went to the shopping mall.
c) Yesterday my parents bought a new car.
d) Yesterday Lara read a book.
e) Yesterday we met our grandparents.
f) Yesterday my best friend and I played tennis.

Lösungen

Test 38 – Das Past Tense: Aussagesätze

A1 **6 Punkte**

a) cried
b) went
c) liked
d) talked
e) died
f) danced

A2 **7 Punkte**

a) ate
b) worked
c) met
d) cleaned
e) watched
f) was
g) caught

A3 **4 Punkte**

a) We did our homework last night.
b) My grandpa worked as a policeman.
c) She visited my parents yesterday.
d) He came home last night.

Test 39 – Das Past Tense: Aussagesätze

A1 **4 Punkte**

a) went; bought
b) saw
c) ate; talked
d) thought

A2 **6 Punkte**

a) Yesterday I played with my cousin.
b) Yesterday we ate pizza.
c) Yesterday it was sunny.
d) Yesterday my parents cooked.
e) Last week I met my aunt.
f) Last year he was in Australia.

Test 40 – Das Past Tense: Aussagesätze

A1 **6 Punkte**

a) was
b) baked
c) called
d) met up
e) danced
f) had

A2 **3 Punkte**

a) + **2)**
b) + **3)**
c) + **1)**

Test 41 – Das Past Tense: Aussagesätze

A1 **6 Punkte**

a) read
b) tried
c) wore
d) slept
e) swam

A2 **3 Punkte**

a) Lisa looked at Ben's answer sheet during the exam.
b) Jenny bought seven bananas at the supermarket today.
c) I cleaned my room already.

A3 **5 Punkte**

a) David did not take a shower after his football match.
b) Lisa wasn't the best student of the last semester.
c) My parents didn't understand what the receptionist at our hotel in Spain was saying.
d) Hannah didn't tell me that you want to meet up at 8 pm.
e) Lisa didn't turn off the light in the living room, did she?

Lösungen

Test 42 – Das Past Tense: Aussagesätze

A1 **5 Punkte**

a) made
b) sang
c) were having
d) spent
e) taught

A2 **4 Punkte**

a) Lizzy brought the pasta salad to the barbeque.
b) Yes, I shut the door to our apartment.
c) I paid 65€ for our dinner tonight.
d) Yes, I spoke French well when I was younger.

A3 **3 Punkte**

a) Last Monday, I sold my old bike.
b) This morning, I drank a lot of apple juice.
c) The maths teacher gave me a good grade.

Test 43 – Das Past Tense: Fragesätze

A1 **7 Punkte**

a) What did you do?
b) Where did you eat?
c) What did you learn?
d) Why did you cry?
e) How did you feel?
f) Where did you sleep?
g) What did you say?

A2 **10 Punkte**

a) Did you see
b) Did he look
c) Did she tell
d) Did they buy
e) Did she smile
f) Did they care
g) Did he clean
h) Did she cook
i) Did they learn
j) Did you sell

Test 44 – Das Past Tense: Fragesätze

A1 **14 Punkte**

a) Did you go to church? –
No, I went to my neighbour.

b) Did you watch a movie? –
No, I watched a football game.

c) Did you see your sister? –
No, I saw my brother.

d) Did you cook spaghetti? –
No, I cooked rice.

e) Did you play hockey? –
No, I played a game.

f) Did you talk to your mother? –
No, I talked to my father.

g) Did you laugh about your friend? –
No, I laughed about my sister.

A2 **7 Punkte**

a) When did they arrive at the house?
b) When did you leave the house?
c) What kind of music did you hear?
d) What did she cook for dinner?
e) Why did you like the city?
f) Why did you go there with your friends?
g) How did you sleep there?

Test 45 – Das Past Tense: Fragesätze

A1 **10 Punkte**

a) When did you buy a new computer?
b) What did I send you yesterday?/
What did you send me yesterday?
c) What did she tell you?
d) Where did you go yesterday?
e) What did he collect when he was young?
f) Where did we wait?
g) Who helped her cook dinner?
h) How did he ask?
i) What did you run last year?
j) When did you run a marathon?

A2 **6 Punkte**

- **a)** Did I call you yesterday?
- **b)** Did we eat pizza?
- **c)** Did you buy a new mobile phone?
- **d)** Did you see the pretty snow globe?
- **e)** Did you ask him about his feelings?
- **f)** Did Sven enjoy his trip to the Bahamas?

Test 46 – Das Past Tense: Verneinte Sätze

A1 **10 Punkte**

- **a)** didn't eat
- **b)** didn't need
- **c)** didn't wash
- **d)** didn't read
- **e)** didn't brush
- **f)** didn't call
- **g)** didn't make
- **h)** didn't love
- **i)** didn't like
- **j)** didn't write

A2 **8 Punkte**

- **a)** didn't play
- **b)** didn't cry
- **c)** didn't go
- **d)** didn't go
- **e)** didn't feel
- **f)** didn't wash
- **g)** didn't meet
- **h)** didn't visit

A3 **5 Punkte**

- **a)** Yesterday he didn't like the food at the restaurant.
- **b)** Yesterday she didn't call her grandma.
- **c)** Yesterday we didn't watch a movie.
- **d)** Yesterday they didn't talk to my grandpa.
- **e)** Last week I didn't buy food at the supermarket.

Test 47 – Das Past Tense: Verneinte Sätze

A1 **4 Punkte**

- **a)** didn't go
didn't feel
- **b)** didn't believe
didn't eat
- **c)** didn't do
- **d)** didn't like;
didn't sleep

A2 **7 Punkte**

- **a)** I didn't go to the shopping mall.
- **b)** My brother didn't play football.
- **c)** My mother didn't cook spaghetti.
- **d)** Kai didn't look after his dog.
- **e)** Jana didn't swim in the ocean.
- **f)** We didn't eat chocolate.
- **g)** They didn't drink a coke.

A3 **6 Punkte**

- **a)** No, they didn't have dinner.
- **b)** No, she didn't drive the car.
- **c)** No, I didn't hear the rain.
- **d)** No, I didn't tell my parents about it.
- **e)** No, she didn't smile.
- **f)** No, he didn't do sports.

Test 48 – Das Past Tense: Verneinte Sätze

A1 **7 Punkte**

- **a)** I didn't talk to my mother about my future.
- **b)** I didn't finish the test very early.
- **c)** He didn't look for his book.
- **d)** She didn't listen to her favourite music.
- **e)** They didn't cook spaghetti and some eggs for dinner.
- **f)** We didn't play football in our garden.
- **g)** She didn't miss the bus yesterday.

A2 **7 Punkte**

a) We didn't play tennis.
b) He didn't go to school.
c) They didn't have fun.
d) You didn't talk to me.
e) She didn't laugh.
f) We didn't eat together.
g) I didn't like chocolate.

A3 **3 Punkte**

a) Yesterday I didn't eat much.
b) He didn't find his favourite game.
c) Yesterday she didn't meet her friend.

Test 49 – Das Past Progressive: Aussagesätze

A1 **10 Punkte**

a) We **were playing** football.
b) Tom **was watching** television.
c) Sandra **was waiting** for the bus.
d) The children **were buying** chocolate.
e) She is playing tennis.
f) They **were living** in Texas.
g) Sarah **was dancing**.
h) Sam is standing beside his bike.
i) It **was raining**.

Bildung des Past Progressive: was/were + Verb -ing

A2 **11 Punkte**

a) was singing
b) were talking
c) were living
d) was swimming
e) were sitting
f) was eating
g) was leaving
h) were discussing
i) was raining
j) were thinking
k) was asking

A3 **8 Punkte**

a) were
b) was
c) was
d) were
e) was
f) were
g) was
h) were

Test 50 – Das Past Progressive: Aussagesätze

A1 **6 Punkte**

a) Cindy was drawing a picture.
b) Grandma Sue was drinking coffee.
c) Baby Ben was crying.
d) Das was reading a paper.
e) Usel was sleeping.
f) Evan was playing with cards.

A2 **7 Punkte**

a) was listening; rang
b) was working
c) was talking; came
d) were playing
e) was watching

Test 51 – Das Past Progressive: Aussagesätze

A1 **8 Punkte**

Individuelle Antworten – hier Musterbeispiele:

a) She was listening to music while he was dancing.

b) He was playing football while Tom was hurting himself.

c) She was reading a book while he was drinking coffee.

d) He was looking on his phone while she was waiting outside.

e) He was sitting on the chair while she was watching TV.

f) She was thinking while he was arriving.

g) She was eating while they were walking.

h) They were swimming while it was raining.

A2 **8 Punkte**

a) The sun was shining while it was raining.

b) Anna was working yesterday at 9 o'clock.

c) They were watching a movie at the cinema.

d) He was sleeping, when she left him.

e) The baby was crying when the music was too loud.

f) The sun was shining yesterday in the morning.

g) Anna was dreaming while she was sleeping.

h) They were eating at 12 o'clock.

Test 52 – Das Past Progressive: Fragesätze

A1 **9 Punkte**

a) Yes, it was.

b) Yes, they were.

c) Yes, he was.

d) Yes, I was.

e) Yes, she was.

f) Yes, they were.

g) Yes, they were.

h) Yes, it was.

i) Yes, she was.

A2 **9 Punkte**

a) Was she

b) Were they

c) Was he

d) Were they

e) Were you

f) Was she

g) Was he

h) Were they

i) Were you

A3 **8 Punkte**

a) Were, I was

b) Was, he was

c) Were, I was

d) Was, she was

e) Was, she was

f) Was, she was

g) Were, I was

h) Were, they were

Test 53 – Das Past Progressive: Fragesätze

A1 **6 Punkte**

a) Was she writing a letter?
b) Was she working when Ben came home?
c) Was he learning for the test?
d) Was the sun shining when they started their walk?
e) Was he leaving the office at 9 o'clock?
f) Was the dog barking when the postman came?

A2 **6 Punkte**

a) Were they visiting the zoo at 3 o'clock?
b) Were Sam and Ben playing soccer when it started raining?
c) Was Lisa reading a book when the doorbell rang?
d) Was she learning for the test?
e) Were they cooking together?
f) Were they driving on the highway when the accident happened?

Test 54 – Das Past Progressive: Fragesätze

A1 **12 Punkte**

a) Were you sleeping, when your parents prepared the breakfast? Yes, I was.
b) Were you going out when it started raining? Yes, I was.
c) Were you dancing when it was 12 o'clock? Yes I was.
d) Were you doing your homework when the sun was shining? No, I wasn't.
e) Were you playing football when your friend arrived? Yes, I was.
f) Were you eating at a restaurant when your mom called. Yes, I was.
g) Were you watching a movie when you fell asleep? Yes, I was.

A2 **10 Punkte**

a) Was Anna driving (her car) when her baby started crying?
b) Was she learning when her dog wanted to go for a walk?
c) Were you sleeping when I called you?
d) Were Tom and Lena meeting at the café?
e) Were you lying on the beach when it was so windy here?
f) Was she working when her husband was sick?
g) Was he watching TV when she knocked on the door?
h) Were they going for a walk, when it started raining?
i) Was Sam waiting for the bus when he met Anna?
j) Were they having breakfast when they saw you?

Test 55 – Das Past Progressive: Verneinte Sätze

A1 **12 Punkte**

a) weren't
b) wasn't
c) wasn't
d) weren't
e) weren't
f) wasn't
g) wasn't
h) wasn't
i) weren't
j) weren't
k) weren't
l) wasn't

A2 **12 Punkte**

a) wasn't leaving
b) wasn't playing
c) wasn't writing
d) wasn't sleeping
e) weren't watching
f) wasn't listening
g) wasn't going
h) wasn't eating
i) weren't waiting
j) weren't talking
k) wasn't calling
l) weren't cleaning

Test 56 – Das Past Progressive: Verneinte Sätze

A1 **9 Punkte**

a) Sam wasn't playing soccer.

b) I wasn't having a shower.

c) She wasn't listening to music.

d) He wasn't packing his bag.

e) The children weren't painting pictures.

f) My mother wasn't preparing dinner.

g) They weren't discussing the book.

h) You weren't talking to the teacher.

i) He wasn't sitting on his chair.

A2 **8 Punkte**

a) No, they weren't having dinner.

b) No, she wasn't playing tennis.

c) No, I wasn't wearing a jacket.

d) No, he wasn't answering my email.

e) No, they weren't leaving early.

f) No, the kids weren't playing outside.

g) No, she wasn't using the computer.

h) No, they weren't driving to the airport.

A3 **3 Punkte**

a) Sam wasn't thinking about the test.

b) They weren't meeting at the café.

c) You weren't reading a book.

Test 57 – Das Past Progressive: Verneinte Sätze

A1 **5 Punkte**

a) I wasn't listening to the radio.

b) They weren't drinking wine.

c) She wasn't reading the book.

d) My sister wasn't driving the car.

e) They weren't waiting for the bus.

A2 **10 Punkte**

a) Were they studying for the test? No, they weren't studying for the test.

b) Was your cousin swimming in the pool? No, he wasn't swimming in the pool.

c) Was Sam baking cookies with Judy? No, Sam wasn't baking cookies with Judy.

d) Were your brothers eating pizza? No, my brothers weren't eating pizza.

e) Was he wearing a t-shirt? No, he wasn't wearing a t-shirt.

Test 70 – Future Tenses: *Das going-to Future*

A1 **6 Punkte**

a) am

b) are

c) is

d) is

e) are

f) are

A2 **4 Punkte**

a) Sarah isn't going to write the exam after lunch.

b) The neighbours aren't going to meet for a barbecue.

c) My brother isn't going to play soccer in the garden.

d) My class mates aren't going to learn for maths together.

A3 **3 Punkte**

a) Yes, the Smiths are going to visit New York City this summer.

b) Yes, dad is going to listen to his favourite band tonight.

c) No, Julia and Stefan aren't going to go to the school ball tonight.

Test 71 – Future Tenses: *Das going-to Future*

A1 **5 Punkte**

a) (+) is going to be
(–) isn't/ is not going to be

b) (+) are going to sleep
(–) aren't/ are not going to sleep

c) (+) is going to say
(–) isn't/ is not going to say

d) (+) are going to go
(–) aren't/ are not going to go

e) (+) am going to hear
(–) am not going to hear

A2 **4 Punkte**

a) Yes, I am going to pass the exams at the end of the year.

b) Yes, the school is going to celebrate an anniversary this autumn.

c) No, she is not going to sing in the choir this semester.

d) No, it is not going to eat fruits for dinner.

A3 **4 Punkte**

a) Is Clara going to become 15 years this Friday?

b) Are your parents going to buy a house at the beach?

c) Are the children going to win the match against the champion?

d) Is the cat going to jump onto the wall?

Test 72 – Future Tenses: *Das going-to Future*

A1 **4 Punkte**

a) richtig
b) richtig
c) falsch
d) richtig

A2 **9 Punkte**

a) are you going to do
b) is going to go
c) are going to be
d) isn't/is not going to bark
e) is going to write
f) aren't/are not going to stay
g) is the plane going to take off
h) is going to take
i) 'm/am going to ask

A3 **5 Punkte**

a) Are you going to do your homework tomorrow night?
b) When is dad going to wash the dishes?
c) How are the students going to solve the problem?
d) Is the doctor going to call the hospital?
e) Where are the children going to meet this weekend?

Test 73 – Das *will* Future

A1 **2 Punkte**

a) ☐ since; for
b) ☒ tomorrow; next month
c) ☐ always; every
d) ☐ last; yesterday
e) ☒ in 2022; the coming year
f) ☐ ever; before

A2 **6 Punkte**

a) Julia and I will talk to them tomorrow.
b) Will you help your father to tidy up the kitchen?
c) They will be back by 8:15 pm.
d) Will the festival take place this summer?
e) My parents will punish me for being late.
f) The Millers will spend Christmas in Sussex this year.

A3 **5 Punkte**

a) They'll read a book.
b) He won't be late.
c) She'll never learn.
d) We won't sing this song.
e) I'll give you the money.

Test 74 – Das *will* Future

A1 5 Punkte

a) (+) will be (–) won't be
b) (+) will sleep (–) won't sleep
c) (+) will say (–) won't say
d) (+) will go (–) won't go
e) (+) will hear (–) won't hear

A2 6 Punkte

a) richtig
b) falsch
c) richtig
d) falsch
e) richtig
f) richtig

A3 5 Punkte

a) richtig
b) richtig
c) falsch
d) richtig
e) falsch

Test 75 – Das *will* Future

A1 6 Punkte

a) richtig
b) falsch
c) richtig
d) falsch
e) richtig
f) richtig

A2 5 Punkte

a) Will it snow?
b) Will she forgive me?
c) What will they learn?
d) Won't the bus wait for us?
e) When will they leave?

A3 3 Punkte

a) falsch
b) richtig
c) richtig

Test 76 – Simple Present oder Present Progressive

A1 12 Punkte

a) present progressive
b) simple present
c) simple present
d) present progressive
e) simple present
f) present progressive
g) simple present
h) present progressive
i) simple present
j) present progressive
k) simple present
l) present progressive

A2 9 Punkte

a) It is raining right now.
b) Sam often listens to jazz music.
c) Anna visits her grandma every Sunday.
d) They usually go to Spain.
e) At the moment she is eating ice cream.
f) They are listening to the teacher right now.
g) She is always late.
h) Listen! Someone is ringing the doorbell.
i) She is still listening to the music.

Test 77 – Simple Present oder Present Progressive

A1 **13 Punkte**

a) are playing
b) speak
c) gets up
d) go
e) Are you watching
f) is reading
g) are going
h) drinks
i) plays
j) watch
k) go
l) are preparing
m) is playing

A2 **8 Punkte**

a) My mother always picks me up after school.
b) She is playing tennis right now.
c) He always learns for the test.
d) They are now standing in front of the house.
e) She is still crying.
f) They are not visiting us today.
g) What are you doing right now?
h) Right now they are dancing.

Test 78 – Simple Present oder Present Progressive

A1 **12 Punkte**

wants; is doing; is staying; take; is; takes; leaves; begins; arrives; offers; are visiting; is enjoying

A2 **6 Punkte**

a) simple present
b) simple present
c) present progressive
d) present progressive
e) present progressive
f) simple present

Test 79 – Simple Past oder Past Progressive

A1 **3 Punkte**

a) past progressive
b) past progressive
c) past progressive
d) simple past
e) past progressive
f) simple past
g) past progressive

A2 **6 Punkte**

a) She was playing guitar when he arrived.

b) While he was waiting, she came in.

c) Sam was having a shower when the baby started crying.

d) First I visited my grandmother then I went to school.

e) She was driving when the accident happened.

f) He was not listening when I started the conversation.

A3 **6 Punkte**

a) came; was playing

b) did; helped

c) was running; happened

Test 80 – Simple Past oder Past Progressive

A1 **22 Punkte**

a) were playing

b) visited

c) came in; sat down; drank

d) was having; visited

e) was watching

f) was reading; started

g) were dancing; stopped

h) was listening

i) was playing; started

j) was doing

k) was going; met

l) were talking; opened

m) were sleeping; came back

A2 **6 Punkte**

a) She woke up, got dressed and made coffee.

b) They were talking when he came in.

c) She was standing outside when he arrived.

d) He was writing a letter when the lights went off.

e) She was learning when her brother started playing his guitar.

f) The teacher was explaining the homework when the girl interrupted him.

Test 81 – Simple Past oder Past Progressive

A1 **12 Punkte**

was driving; ran; was texting; was shining; felt; went; was listening; heard; was tumbling; turned; saw; was coming

A2 **4 Punkte**

a) Were you smoking a cigarette when you started to cough?

b) Sandra wasn't knitting on the sofa at 10 o'clock in the morning.

c) Anton wasn't dancing when I arrived.

d) Did the dog catch the cat?

A3 **4 Punkte**

a) went; bought

b) was telling, ran

c) was watching; was making

d) was raining; left

Test 82 – *will*-Future oder *going to*-Future

A1 **6 Punkte**

Will Future	Going-to-Future
Künftiges Geschehen, das nicht beeinflussbar ist	logische Schlussfolgerung
Vermutungen	Absicht im Moment des Sprechens bereits vorhanden
spontane Entscheidungen	Keine spontane Entscheidung

A2 **10 Punkte**

a) ☒ Wait a minute. I'll help you.
☐ Wait a minute. I'm going to help you.

b) ☒ Tom will be 15 next Monday.
☐ Tom is going to be 15 next Monday.

c) ☐ Look outside! It will be rain.
☒ Look outside! It is going to rain.

d) ☒ I think she will marry him.
☐ I think she is going to marry him.

e) ☐ I will visit you tomorrow.
☒ I'm going to visit you tomorrow.

f) ☐ We will go to Spain next year.
☒ We are going to go to Spain next year.

g) ☒ I think the train will arrive at 9 o'clock.
☐ I think the train is going to arrive at 9 o'clock.

h) ☐ Sam came home late. He will be tired tomorrow.
☒ Sam came home late. He is going to be tired tomorrow.

i) ☐ It's cold. The streets will be slippery.
☒ It's cold. The streets are going to be slippery.

j) ☒ I think they will close at 8 o'clock.
☐ I think they are going to close at 8 o'clock.

Test 83 – *will*-Future oder *going to*-Future

A1 **14 Punkte**

a) am going to do
b) will meet
c) will rain
d) will go
e) are going to visit
f) will visit
g) going to meet
h) am going to leave
i) will be
j) will like
k) will help
l) will be
m) am going to give
n) is going to be

A2 **8 Punkte**

a) I think they will go to the cinema.
b) I am going to meet her at 8 o'clock.
c) We are going to meet my mother tomorrow.
d) Maybe she will win the match.
e) I hope I will pass the test.
f) We are going to have a party next week.
g) I am going to go to Berlin on Monday.
h) I think they will be friends.

Test 84 – *will*-Future oder *going to*-Future

A1 **8 Punkte**

a) I think they'll will like each other.
b) I'm going to play soccer tomorrow.
c) It is raining. It's going to be wet outside.
d) Wait! I'll go with you.
e) I'm going to leave at 8 o'clock.
f) I hope the test will be easy.
g) We're going to go to the cinema tomorrow evening.
h) I'm going to visit my grandmother on Sunday.

A2 **5 Punkte**

a) I'm going to meet friends on Saturday.

b) She will arrive in 3 hours.

c) Yes, I'll help you.

d) I think, this idea will be great.

e) I'm going to play football.

Test 85 – Die modalen Hilfsverben *can* und *can't*

A1 **5 Punkte**

a) can

b) can't

c) can

d) can't

e) can

A2 **10 Punkte**

a) Yes, I can read. / No, I can't read.

b) Yes, he can speak. / No, he can't speak.

c) Yes, she can write. / No, she can't write.

d) Yes, I can climb trees. / No, I can't climb trees.

e) Yes, he can play football. / No, he can't play football.

A3 **5 Punkte**

a) can't

b) can

c) can

d) can't

e) can't

Test 86 – Die modalen Hilfsverben *can* und *can't*

A1 **5 Punkte**

a) can't

b) can

c) can't

d) can

e) can't

A2 **5 Punkte**

a) can; can't

b) can

c) can; can't

A3 **9 Punkte**

a) can't; can

b) he can't; he can

c) I can't; I can

d) they can

e) he can't; he can

Test 87 – Die modalen Hilfsverben *can* und *can’t*

A1 **5 Punkte**

a) can
b) can
c) Can
d) can
e) can‘t

A2 **10 Punkte**

a) Can some fish walk? – Yes, they can.
b) Can Peter swim? – No, he can’t.
c) Can Oliver ride a bicycle? – Yes, he can.
d) Can you speak Chinese? – No, I can’t.
e) Can you play the guitar? – Yes, I can.

A3 **7 Punkte**

a) can
b) can’t
c) can’t
d) can’t
e) can’t
f) can
g) Can

Test 88 – Die modalen Hilfsverben *must* und *needn’t*

A1 **3 Punkte**

a) mustn’t
b) must
c) needn‘t

A2 **7 Punkte**

a) must repair the wheel
b) needn’t buy more cake
c) needn’t write the test
d) must buy a new t-shirt
e) must do your homework
f) needn’t call them
g) must play in the house

Test 89 – Die modalen Hilfsverben *must* und *needn’t*

A1 **4 Punkte**

a) + **3)**
b) + **1)**
c) + **2)**
d) + **4)**

A2 **10 Punkte**

a) needn’t
b) mustn’t
c) mustn’t
d) needn’t
e) mustn’t
f) needn’t
g) needn’t
h) needn’t
i) mustn’t
j) mustn’t

A3 **6 Punkte**

a) needn’t
b) must
c) mustn’t
d) mustn’t
e) must
f) needn’t

Test 90 – Die modalen Hilfsverben *must* und *needn't*

A1 **6 Punkte**

a) must
b) mustn't
c) needn't
d) must
e) mustn't
f) needn't

A2 **6 Punkte**

a) needn't hurry
b) mustn't forget
c) must go – needn't go
d) must write
e) needn't walk
f) mustn't open

A3 **7 Punkte**

must; needn't; needs; must; mustn't; needn't; must

Test 91 – Die modalen Hilfsverben: *may* und *might*

A1 **2 Punkte**

a) **3)** Might ist die höflichere und auch formellere Form.

b) **2)** Might klingt etwas unwahrscheinlicher und wird deshalb mit dürften übersetzt; May wird mit dürfen übersetzt.

A2 **2 Punkte**

b) might not; **e)** may not

A3 **6 Punkte**

a) Today we have no homework. We **may** play football.
b) **May** I visit you today?
c) Might I go to the bathroom, please? Yes, you **might**.
d) My dad **might** be on time today, but usually he is 10 minutes late.
e) I **may** be at home the whole afternoon, I don't have a lot to do.
f) **May** I ask you a question?

Test 92 – Die modalen Hilfsverben: *may* und *might*

A1 **9 Punkte**

a) May
b) may
c) May/Might
d) may
e) might
f) might not
g) may not
h) may
i) might

A2 **4 Punkte**

a) We may not do our homework with a red pen.
b) We may miss the train, because we are very late.
c) However, we might catch the train, if the train is late as well.
d) It may rain today. It looks very cloudy.

A3 **4 Punkte**

a) Yes, you might.
b) No, you may not.
c) Yes, you may.
d) No, you might not.

Test 93 – Die modalen Hilfsverben: *may* und *might*

A1 **6 Punkte**

a) may
b) might
c) may
d) might
e) may
f) might

A2 **4 Punkte**

a) We may not walk to school today.
b) May I put my bag here?
c) May I also have a piece of cake?
d) It may/might snow tomorrow.

A3 **7 Punkte**

a) Might I open the window, please?
b) May I borrow your book today?
c) We may/might also play tennis.
d) Jenny may/might also be in her room.
e) Tom may drive to school by car today.
f) Mum may/might not have time today to help you with your homework.
g) Do you see the clouds? Tonight it may rain.

Test 94 – Das Verb *to be*

A1 **8 Punkte**

a) is
b) are
c) is
d) am
e) are
f) are
g) is
h) am

A2 **8 Punkte**

a) 's
b) 're
c) 'm
d) 're
e) 's
f) 's
g) 're
h) 'm

A3 **8 Punkte**

a) is
b) are
c) are
d) is
e) is
f) am
g) is
h) am

Test 95 – Das Verb *to be*

A1 **7 Punkte**

a) They're
b) It's
c) She's
d) I'm
e) He's
f) we're
g) you're

A2 **6 Punkte**

a) 'm not
b) aren't
c) 'm not
d) isn't
e) isn't
f) aren't

A3 **12 Punkte**

a) Is he 15 years old?
b) Are you in the garden?
c) Are your parents German?
d) Is it warm today?
e) Is Sophia your friend?
f) Is your dog black?

Test 96 – Das Verb *to be*

A1 **13 Punkte**

a) am; am; am
b) is; is
c) are
d) am; is; is
e) are; am
f) am
g) is

A2 **5 Punkte**

a) was; was
b) was; was
c) were

A3 **5 Punkte**

a) Hello, how are you?
b) I am fine.
c) I am from Germany.
d) I was in school yesterday / Yesterday I was in school.
e) We were at a concert.

Test 97 – Der Imperativ

A1 **10 Punkte**

a) Befehlsform; Aufforderungen, Warnungen, Bitten
b) Grundform des Verbes
c) Personenzahl
d) Verneinung; Hilfsverb
e) please
f) Aufforderungssätze
g) *let us*; *let is*.

A2 **10 Punkte**

a) Ruf mich an, wenn du zu Hause bist.
b) Spring da nicht hinein!
c) Reiche mir bitte die Butter.
d) Lasst uns hineingehen.
e) Lasst uns nicht ihre Aufmerksamkeit auf uns ziehen.
f) Schließe bitte das Fenster.
g) Hör nicht auf ihn!
h) Sei leise.
i) Hör mir zu / Hör auf mich.
j) Gib mir bitte mehr Zeit.

Test 98 – Der Imperativ

A1 **9 Punkte**

a) Open the window.
b) Clean your room.
c) Eat your sandwiches.
d) Help your mother.
e) Do your homework.
f) Wash your car.
g) Draw a picture for your dad.
h) Get married.
i) Do it.

*Optional kann immer ein "Please" vor die Sätze gestellt werden.

A2 **7 Punkte**

a) Don't put on the t-shirt.
b) Don't drink alcohol.
c) Don't play loud music.
d) Don't walk on the road.
e) Don't get lost.
f) Don't do anything bad.
g) Don't walk away.

Test 99 – Der Imperativ

A1 **7 Punkte**

a) Let's go to the beach. / Let's do something else.
b) Let's buy pizza.
c) Listen to me.
d) Let's all go outside.
e) Open the door.
f) Eat the sand cake.
g) Let's eat the sand cake.

A2 **8 Punkte**

a) Join
b) Don't look
c) Go
d) Don't lie
e) Call
f) Turn
g) Bring
h) Don't play

Test 100 – Die Personalpronomen: Subjekt- und Objektform

A1 **8 Punkte**

a) you
b) you
c) she
d) he
e) he
f) I
g) they
h) we

A2 **8 Punkte**

a) her
b) it
c) him
d) it
e) them
f) it
g) me
h) them

A3 **5 Punkte**

a) you
b) she
c) he
d) we
e) they

Test 101 – Die Personalpronomen: Subjekt- und Objektform

A1 **5 Punkte**

a) The Johnsons have got a dog. They feed it every day.
b) Lisa has got pens. She uses them often.
c) Lars has got a new car. He drives it every day.
d) Mum sees an old woman. She wants to help her.
e) Sandra likes flowers. She has got five of them.

A2 **16 Punkte**

a) She, it
b) They
c) I
d) it
e) He
f) She
g) We
h) it
i) She; his; she
j) We, you
k) we
l) He

Test 102 – Die Personalpronomen: Subjekt- und Objektform

A1 **3 Punkte**

a) to visit **her**
b) **She** has to
c) **Her** mother is

A2 **6 Punkte**

a) us
b) them
c) him
d) It
e) her
f) it

A3 **6 Punkte**

a) me/her
b) it
c) him
d) us
e) it
f) me

Test 103 – Die Possessivpronomen

A1 **9 Punkte**

a) mine
b) yours
c) hers
d) ours
e) his
f) hers
g) his
h) hers
i) mine

A2 **7 Punkte**

a) your; my; your; my
b) their; my; your

A3 **5 Punkte**

a) his
b) my
c) their
d) my
e) her

Test 104 – Die Possessivpronomen

A1 **4 Punkte**

a) mine
b) yours
c) his
d) her

A2 **6 Punkte**

a) their
b) her
c) his
d) their
e) my
f) my

A3 **4 Punkte**

a) Lukas, is it **your** camera? No, this isn't **my** camera. I think it's his camera.

b) Karin, is it your pizza? Yes, it's **my** pizza.

c) Stop, why are you wearing **my** clothes, Konrad? – Because **my** clothes are dirty.

d) This is **my** room, please don't sit on **my** bed and stop eating **your** chocolate.

Test 105 – Die Possessivpronomen

A1 **5 Punkte**

a) my
b) your
c) her
d) mine
e) his

A2 **10 Punkte**

your; our; our; our; your; my; her; her; my; their

A3 **4 Punkte**

a) our; yours
b) my; your
c) his; her
d) my; yours

Test 106 – Demonstrativpronomen

A1 **6 Punkte**

a) These
b) These
c) This
d) This
e) This
f) These

A2 **6 Punkte**

a) Those
b) That
c) That
d) Those
e) That
f) Those

A3 **7 Punkte**

a) this; it; that; it
b) this; that; it

Test 107 – Demonstrativpronomen

A1 **6 Punkte**

a) this
b) that
c) These
d) That
e) Those
f) That

A2 **6 Punkte**

a) this
b) Those
c) that
d) this
e) those
f) this

A3 **4 Punkte**

a) I can see this girl and that woman
b) I can see this car and that truck
c) I can see these flowers and that tree
d) I can see these dogs and those cats

Test 108 – Demonstrativpronomen

A1 **5 Punkte**

a) that
b) those
c) those
d) this
e) these

A2 **5 Punkte**

a) These
b) That
c) Those
d) This
e) this

A3 **5 Punkte**

a) That
b) These
c) This
d) Those
e) That

Test 109 – Die Reflexivpronomen

A1 **8 Punkte**

Singular	1. Person	I	myself
	2. Person	you	yourself
	3. Person	he	himself
		she	herself
		it	itself
Plural	1. Person	we	ourselves
	2. Person	you	yourselves
	3. Person	they	themselves

A2 **12 Punkte**

		wahr	falsch
a)	Reflexivpronomen werden auch rückbezügliche Fürwörter genannt.	☒	
b)	Mit Reflexivpronomen kann betont werden, dass eine Person etwas selbst tut.	☒	
c)	Reflexivpronomen können stellvertretend für das Subjekt in einem Satz stehen.		☒
d)	Reflexivpronomen können weggelassen werden.		☒
e)	Im Englischen steht in der Einzahl -self und in der Mehrzahl -selves am Ende der Reflexivpronomen.	☒	
f)	Reflexivpronomen beziehen sich auf das Subjekt im Satz.	☒	
g)	Reflexivpronomen werden verwendet, wenn man betonen möchte, dass jemand etwas ohne fremde Hilfe geschafft hat.	☒	
h)	Im Englischen gibt es weniger Verben, die reflexiv verwendet werden, als im Deutschen.	☒	

i)	Reflexivpronomen stehen immer direkt hinter dem Subjekt, auf das sie sich beziehen.		☒
j)	Reflexivpronomen werden auch besitzanzeigende Fürwörter genannt.		☒
k)	Reflexivpronomen werden verwendet, wenn Subjekt und Objekt in einem Satz dieselbe Person haben.	☒	
l)	Um auszudrücken, dass etwas gegenseitig oder miteinander geschieht, wird statt der Reflexivpronomen each other verwendet.	☒	

Test 110 – Die Reflexivpronomen

A1 **6 Punkte**

yourself; ourselves; herself; yourselves; myself; himself

A2 **14 Punkte**

1e, 2j, 3l, 4f, 5k, 6i, 7d, 8a, 9b, 10m, 11h, 12g, 13n, 14c

A3 **7 Punkte**

a) to behave oneself
b) to cut oneself
c) to dry oneself
d) to enjoy oneself
e) to express oneself
f) to hurt oneself
g) to introduce oneself

Test 111 – Die Reflexivpronomen

A1 **26 Punkte**

a) Let me introduce myself, my name is Mrs. Marshall and I am your new English teacher.

b) I love art. It is a way to express myself.

c) Enjoy yourself/yourselves at the party tonight. I heard they invited a surprise guest.

d) Patrick doesn't want to hurt himself, so he is very careful.

e) Girls, you can be really proud of yourselves.

f) The president himself talked to the people on the street.

g) He doesn't need our help. He can defend himself.

h) My Mum cut herself while making dinner.

i) Did you eat the whole cake yourself?

j) Mary taught herself to change her car tires.

k) The dirty dishes don't wash themselves.

l) The child cannot remember the name of the street.

m) He didn't sleep very well last night, so today he feels tired.

n) She brought a birthday cake for herself.

o) Children, please behave yourselves during class.

p) We will move the furniture ourselves.

q) The candle went out by itself.

r) After taking a shower you have to dry yourself.

s) We are talking to each other on the phone.

t) I can't help you any longer, you have to finish your homework yourself.

u) He felt very sad when she left him.

v) I can open the door myself.

w) She cuts her own hair.

x) We fixed our bikes all by ourselves.

y) The cat licked itself.

z) Sebastian can't see himself in the mirror, because he is a vampire.

Test 112 – Abschlusstest

A1 **4 Punkte**

a) On Sundays I take out my dog to play.
b) Does it rain in England every day?
c) They don't like to ride their old bikes.
d) We are not driving to the city right now.

A2 **6 Punkte**

a) doesn't play – wins
b) don't watch – am doing
c) likes – want
d) Are – listening – playing
e) read – reads
f) don't go – are being

A3 **6 Punkte**

a) Was playing – arrived
b) became – was travelling
c) did – go
d) were – waiting – came
e) said – wasn't feeling – talked
f) were – doing – heard

A4 **4 Punkte**

a) go – was having
b) makes – ate – was working
c) came – was being
d) do – want – take

A5 **6 Punkte**

a) my/our – he
b) I – my – our – we
c) they – them
d) I – your – you – me
e) my – you – it
f) theirs/it – ours

Zusatzaufgaben

A6 **5 Punkte**

a) am
b) is
c) is
d) are, am
e) is, is

A7 **10 Punkte**

a) His; they
b) My; your
c) My; you; her
d) His
e) Mine
f) Our; he
g) Their
h) Yours
i) Mine
j) You

A8 **4 Punkte**

a) Are laughing
b) Is listening
c) Are talking
d) Am reading

A9 **4 Punkte**

a) Were playing
b) Was doing
c) Were visiting
d) Was cooking

A10 **6 Punkte**

a) Are playing
b) Goes
c) Writes; is writing
d) Is listening
e) Are leaving
f) Write

Notizen

Notizen

Bitte hier ausfüllen

und in der nächstgelegenen Schülerhilfe vor Ort abgeben.
Weitere Infos über die Schülerhilfe unter www.schuelerhilfe.de.

Vorname	Name
PLZ	Ort
Straße	Geburtsdatum
Telefon	E-Mail